THE CUBAN AMERICAN
FAMILY
ALBUM

THE CUBAN AMERICAN
FAMILY
ALBUM

DOROTHY AND THOMAS HOOBLER
Introduction by Oscar Hijuelos

OXFORD UNIVERSITY PRESS • NEW YORK • OXFORD

Authors' Note: The accounts in this book have been taken from many different sources. Some people spelled their names in customary Spanish fashion, with accent marks. Others wrote their names without accents. We have left each spelling as the author wished it to appear.

Oxford University Press

Oxford New York
Athens Auckland Bangkok Bogotá Bombay
Buenos Aires Calcutta Cape Town Dar es Salaam
Delhi Florence Hong Kong Istanbul Karachi
Kuala Lumpur Madras Madrid Melbourne
Mexico City Nairobi Paris Singapore
Taipei Tokyo Toronto

and associated companies in
Berlin Ibadan

Design: Sandy Kaufman
Layout: Valerie Sauers
Consultant: Yolanda Prieto, Professor of Sociology, Ramapo College of New Jersey

Published by Oxford University Press, Inc.,
198 Madison Avenue, New York, New York 10016

Oxford is a registered trademark of Oxford University Press

Library of Congress Cataloging-in-Publication Data

Hoobler, Dorothy.
The Cuban American family album / Dorothy and Thomas Hoobler;
introduction by Oscar Hijuelos
p. cm. — (American family albums)
Summary: Interviews, excerpts from diaries and letters, newspaper accounts, profiles of famous
individuals, and pictures from family albums portray the Cuban American experience.
1. Cuban American families—Juvenile literature. 2. Cuban Americans—History—Juvenile literature.
[1. Cuban Americans—History.]
I. Hoobler, Thomas. II. Title. III. Series.
E184.C97H66   1996
973'.04687291—dc20   95-38103
                                                            CIP
                                                            AC

ISBN 0-19-508132-3 (lib. ed.); ISBN 0-19-510340-8 (trade ed.); ISBN 0-19-510172-3 (series, lib. ed.)

9 8 7 6 5 4 3 2 1

Printed in the United States of America
on acid-free paper

Cover: Oliver and Janet Garcia (standing in the center) with friends and family at their wedding
Frontispiece: Rosie Rodriguez at her *quinceañera*

CONTENTS

A girl waits at a Red Cross–operated Cuban refugee center in Florida in 1963.

INTRODUCTION

by Oscar Hijuelos

Having grown up in Manhattan during the 1950s and '60s, in a city jumping with ethnic energies, it's hard for me to offer a self-portrait in a few words that would reflect *my endless feelings* about being Cuban and my family past. As a writer, being Cuban and New York–born at the same time has meant looking out and beyond my own circumstances, and marveling at the beauty of a Latin culture and heritage that has given the world many remarkable individuals. I'm talking not only about movie stars like Andy Garcia or grand divas like the magnificent Celia Cruz, but ordinary folks for the most part—*mi gente*—whom I have encountered in every walk of life, spread wide over this nation; exuberant, lively beings who just have that Cuban edge, a certain soulfulness and love for life that might best be encapsulated in a single word—*duende.*

My mother and father, Magdalena and Pascual Hijuelos, began their life in this country as a young couple in 1943. Like many other Latinos of their generation, they had their share of both suffering and glories; my father, fresh from a farm in Oriente Province, had come to New York to join two of his sisters, Borja and Maya, in an ethnically mixed Upper West

At Coney Island around 1954, Pascual Hijuelos and his wife, Magdalena, pose with sons Oscar (holding his father's hand) and José.

Side Manhattan neighborhood, settling into the very apartment where my mother still lives to this day. Perhaps my father had come only to visit or perhaps he had journeyed north for more opportunity and excitement to partake in, as he and many others of the postwar period did, a kind of mambo highlife, with my mother.

In any event, their lives and that of their generation of pre-Castro Cubans is something that I've tried to understand through my work; though I am best known for having written *The Mambo Kings Play Songs of Love* (about two Cuban musicians in New York in the 1950s), much of what my parents' generation went through has been a source of inspiration for my other novels.

Until his death in 1969, my father worked as a cook at the Biltmore Hotel. My mother, now in her early eighties, Cuban as ever, passes her days writing poetry (about Cuba and subjects close to her heart) and keeping up with a lively social life. I have an older brother, Joseph or José, who is a painter and teacher, and a great number of cousins, living both here and in Cuba. Some of my American cousins arrived in the States long before 1960, and others afterward, but they have all shared certain things in common, virtues that I consider quite Cuban—a powerful work ethic and strong sense of shared responsibility, family pride and affection.

The Russian writer Boris Pasternak once likened the presence of religion in a novel to a stove or fireplace in a cold house in winter: I would like to adapt this idea slightly; where there are Cubans, there will be much warmth, life, and amazing energy.

Oscar Hijuelos

Novelist Oscar Hijuelos was born to Cuban immigrants in 1951 on the Upper West Side of New York City, a neighborhood that continues to influence and shape his writing.

After receiving his B.A. and M.A. degrees from the City College of New York, Hijuelos earned his living by working for a mass-transit advertising agency. Before and after hours, however, he began work on his first novel, Our House in the Last World. His debut was a success and won him several awards and grants. These allowed him to leave his job and write his second novel, The Mambo Kings Play Songs of Love, which won the 1990 Pulitzer Prize for fiction. It was a national and international bestseller. In 1993, Hijeulos published his third novel, The Fourteen Sisters of Emilio Montez O'Brien, which also became a national bestseller. The Chicago Tribune remarked: "Nobody writes about sensuality, nostalgia, and matters of the heart more exuberantly than Oscar Hijuelos." Mr. Ives' Christmas, published in 1995, also received rave reviews.

Although he travels the world, Oscar Hijuelos still makes his home in New York City.

This photo, taken around 1955, is the only one of Oscar Hijuelos in Cuba. He sits at the center, with his mother and brother to the left, at the home of his Aunt Mercedes in Holguín.

Oscar Hijuelos and actor Armand Assante in California during the filming of The Mambo Kings Play Songs of Love in 1992.

During the 1995 Christmas holidays in New York, Oscar (left), his nephew Matthew (middle), and his brother, José, celebrate with their mother, waving in the background.

Life could be elegant for upper-class Cubans. This family enjoys an afternoon at home on the patio in the early years of the 20th century. Their gardeners tend plants in pots high above.

CHAPTER ONE

THE OLD COUNTRY

have never seen anything so beautiful," wrote Christopher Columbus when he arrived at the island of Cuba on October 27, 1492. He also marveled at the bounty of the island. The native Cubans grew many kinds of crops the Spaniards had never seen before, such as pineapples, tomatoes, corn, and tobacco.

Within a few years, Spain realized the strategic importance of Cuba as the key to the New World. Located at the entrance of the Gulf of Mexico, Cuba is less than 100 miles from both the southern tip of Florida and the coast of Mexico. Across the Caribbean Sea to the south lies the continent of South America. Cuba was an ideal site for the Spanish to establish a base for their expeditions of conquest throughout the Americas.

Tragically, that fact doomed the native Cubans. In 1511, the Spanish conquistador Diego Velázquez de Cuéllar invaded the island and enslaved its people. Within 50 years, virtually all of the original inhabitants had died from cruel treatment or disease. The Spanish brought in slaves from Africa to replace the native Cubans as menial laborers. These slaves were put to work building sugar and coffee plantations.

Slavery in Cuba was somewhat different from slavery in the United States. Customarily, Cuban slaveholders freed the children they had with African women. Intermarriage between free Africans and Europeans was also relatively common in Cuba, compared to the United States. Thus, Cubans of African descent began to play an important role in the island's affairs. African religions, folklore, and music became embedded in Cuban culture.

In the first quarter of the 19th century, revolutions broke out against Spanish rule in the New World. The Spanish colonies of South America and Mexico won their independence from Spain.

Cuban *criollos* (people of European descent born in Cuba) also resented Spanish rule. But for a variety of reasons, Cubans did not overthrow Spanish rule at the same time that South Americans and Mexicans did. Cubans of European descent were outnumbered by African slaves. Thus, the *criollos* feared that independence would bring about a slave insurrection like the one that had brought a black-dominated government to the neighboring country of Haiti.

To satisfy the Cubans' yearning for greater freedom, Spain relaxed some of the trade regulations that

kept Cubans from selling their sugar, coffee, and tobacco to other nations. In addition, Cubans were permitted to send representatives to the Spanish Cortes, or parliament.

In 1845, Spain passed a law that forbade any further importation of slaves to Cuba, and also ordered freedom for all slaves imported after 1820. Cuban *criollos* were unwilling to comply with the law. Many felt that the best course of action was for Cuba to become part of the United States, where slavery was still legal.

This idea won support in the United States as well. Slave owners in the southern United States favored the annexation of Cuba as a way of increasing the number of slave states. In 1848, U.S. President James K. Polk offered to buy Cuba from Spain for $100 million. Six years later, President Franklin Pierce raised the offer to $130 million. Spain refused both offers, unwilling to relinquish what was by that time its most important territory in the New World.

In October 1868, a group of sugar planters and cattle ranchers met at the town of Yara to proclaim Cuban independence. *El Grito de Yara* (the cry of Yara) attracted the support of Cubans of all classes and races. Carlos Manuel de Céspedes, the leader of the independence movement, was a plantation owner of partial African descent.

Spain responded harshly, sending an army to put down the rebellion. What followed is remembered as the Ten Years' War, in which more than 200,000 Cubans and Spaniards perished. (The population of Cuba at that time was about 1.5 million.) The Cubans turned to guerrilla warfare, burning the plantations and sugar mills in most of the eastern half of the island. After a decade of devastating conflict, Spain ended the war by promising sweeping government reforms.

However, Spain never fulfilled most of its promises, and it required the Cuban people to pay for the immense destruction of property that occurred during the war. Though the slaves were freed in 1880, they were required to work for their former owners for six more years.

Cuba's three major sources of income—tobacco, coffee, and sugar—all suffered a decline after the war. The coffee industry never recovered, and some of the Cuban cigar manufacturers moved their operations to Florida. To rebuild its sugar industry, Cuba had to ask companies in the United States to supply the capital. As a result, by 1895 fewer than 20 percent of the Cuban sugar mills were owned by Cubans, and 95 percent of the sugar produced on the island went to the United States.

One of those who fought in the Ten Years' War was a 16-year-old boy named José Martí. Taken prisoner, he was exiled to Spain. Along with thousands of others who had fled Cuba during and after the Ten Years' War, Martí continued to work for Cuban independence.

While living in New York City in 1892, Martí and other veterans of the Ten Years' War founded the Partido Revolucionario Cubano (PRC). With funds raised from Cubans in the United States, the PRC assembled an army and invaded Cuba in April 1895.

The fighting was even more vicious than in the Ten Years' War.

Cubans from rural areas of the island took their products to cities to sell. This man leads a horse-drawn cart filled with plantains around 1910.

The Spaniards rounded up civilians suspected of supporting the rebels and put them in internment camps, where many died. Though Martí was killed early in the war, patriot leaders such as the Cuban African Antonio Maceo carried on the fight. In October 1897, the Spanish governor offered peace terms, but he would not grant the rebels' demand for independence.

At that point, the United States became involved in the conflict. President William McKinley sent the battleship *Maine* into Havana harbor to protect the lives and property of U.S. citizens in Cuba. On February 15, 1898, two explosions sent the *Maine* to the bottom of the harbor, along with 260 crew members. Sensational accounts in American newspapers of the day blamed the Spanish. On April 25, Congress declared war against Spain.

The war lasted less than four months. When it was over, the Cuban people found that they had exchanged one foreign ruler for another. As Spanish troops left the island on January 1, 1899, the United States set up a military government to supervise the transition to independence.

In November 1900, Cubans were permitted to elect delegates to a constitutional convention. To make the constitution acceptable to the United States, the delegates had to adopt several provisions known as the Platt Amendment (after Orville H. Platt, who introduced it in the U.S. Senate). The United States was granted the right to intervene when necessary to preserve Cuban independence.

Cubans finally celebrated their independence in May 1902, when Tomás Estrada Palma took office as the nation's first president. He negotiated a trade treaty with the United States that reduced tariffs on sugar. From then until the 1960s, sugar was Cuba's most profitable crop and the United States its biggest customer. During Estrada Palma's term the United States exercised its right under the

Platt Amendment to build a huge naval base at Guantánamo Bay.

In 1905, Estrada Palma won reelection, but his opponent charged that the election was rigged and started a rebellion. The United States once more sent its troops to take control of Cuba's government. They remained until 1909. The pattern of U.S. intervention in Cuban affairs was repeated several times between then and 1923.

In the years that followed, Cuba's political leaders often used their power to enrich themselves. Electoral fraud became commonplace, and rival candidates frequently appealed to the U.S. ambassador to settle the disputes. Naturally, most Cubans resented the fact that the United States had so much power over their country.

General Gerardo Machado became president in 1925. Machado made himself a dictator; he used terror and military force to quell opposition, and he suspended the freedoms of press and speech guaranteed by the constitution.

In 1933, U.S. President Franklin Roosevelt sent an ambassador to Cuba who refused to recognize the dictator. With U.S. warships in the harbor, though no troops were landed, Machado left the country. The following year, to the cheers of Cubans, the United States signed a treaty that nullified the Platt Amendment.

For most of the next 10 years a Cuban military officer named Fulgencio Batista controlled the government. In 1944, when a reform candidate took office, Batista fled the island. But he returned in 1952, again seizing power. Batista won the support of a majority of the people by identifying himself with *los humildes* (the lowly). Indeed, some of Batista's ancestors were African slaves, a fact that kept him from being accepted by Havana's most exclusive club, whose members took pride in their "pure" Spanish ancestry.

Sadly, however, Batista's performance in office was as bad as

Friends gather around the cake in a middle-class home in Havana to celebrate a birthday in the 1950s.

any of his predecessors'. He encouraged foreign investment in Cuba but divided the proceeds among his friends and family. With Batista's approval, organized crime elements from the United States operated casinos and brothels in Havana, turning it into a playground for rich Americans.

In December 1956, a Cuban political exile named Fidel Castro landed in Cuba with a small force of rebels. Castro soon won the support of Cubans both rich and poor, who believed that anything was preferable to Batista's government. On January 1, 1959, Batista and his family fled.

Within a year, tensions between Cuba and the United States mounted. The Castro government nationalized plantations, factories, and estates to bring the economy under government control. In 1960, the United States broke diplomatic relations with Cuba. Soon after that, in 1961, Castro declared that the revolution underway would follow a communist path.

The U.S. Central Intelligence Agency helped to plan an invasion of Cuba by Cuban exiles who had fled to the United States. However, when the invasion began on April 17, 1961, President John F. Kennedy refused to support it with U.S. air power. The invasion was an embarrassing failure.

The following year, the Soviet Union, which was now Cuba's strongest ally and trading partner, started to build missile bases in Cuba. President Kennedy threatened to attack Soviet ships carrying missiles if they did not turn back. For a few days, the United States and the Soviet Union seemed on the brink of nuclear war. However, the Soviet ships finally retreated in return for Kennedy's pledge not to invade Cuba.

Since the Cuban Missile Crisis, the United States has tried to dislodge Cuba's communist government through economic pressure. Despite these efforts, Castro remained in power and ruled Cuba longer than any other leader in its history.

Map of Cuba showing UNITED STATES, FLORIDA, Atlantic Ocean, Gulf of Mexico, Miami, THE BAHAMAS, Havana, Matanzas, Santa Clara, Camagüey, PINAR DEL RIO, HAVANA, MATANZAS, LAS VILLAS, CAMAGÜEY, ORIENTE, Pinar del Río, ISLE OF PINES, CUBA, Santiago de Cuba, HAITI, Caribbean Sea

The mandolin and the guitar were popular in the Spanish colonies as well as in Spain. Music helped to while away the time on this Cuban ranch.

LIFE IN CUBA

Jose Ramon Sanfeliz was born in a suburb of Havana in 1870. Later he came to the United States, where he worked in a cigar factory. He spoke to an interviewer in the 1930s about his early life.

I learned my alphabet, and first preliminary schooling from my mother and my aunt. When I was ten years of age I was put to work at the cigar factory of Hijos de Cabaña y Cajal, of Dragones #6, Havana. I worked here as a stripper [a worker who removed the center stem from the tobacco leaf]. In the afternoon when I was through with work, I would go home, eat, and then go to night school....

At twelve years of age I went to the sugar mill known as "La Concordia" where my father was working as foreman. I remained here until I was 14 years of age.

On August of the year 1884, I was contracted [giving two years of free labor in return for being taught the trade] as apprentice cigar-maker at the factory of "El Nuevo Mundo" of Ramirez and Villamil. I distinctly remember this place as I received many beatings, many blows, and very poor food. I had to remain here two whole years which seemed to me more like two ages.

As a very old man, former slave Esteban Montejo described the Afro-Cuban community in the town of Remedios in the 1890s.

The Negroes in Remedios had two clubs: a recreation centre on the corner of Brigadier Gonzalez Street, and one for religious rites. During Holy Week the recreation club had an all-Negro dance band. *Danzones* [slow dances] were very popular in those days, and Negroes danced them in the streets as well as in the halls. The band didn't only play for Negroes. Sometimes they went along to the Tertulia, the whites' club, and played there for a bit. The musicians were well paid....

People in Remedios, as in all the other nearby villages, breakfasted early, and the table was cleared by half-past six or seven. The poor people breakfasted even earlier, especially the country folk, on coffee and sweet potato—delicious sweet potato cooked the African way, in hot cinders. They had lunch at eleven-thirty, and a well-off household always had bread, butter and wine....

People drank a lot of coffee, and every household had its big black coffee-pots and roasted its own beans, and if they didn't have a coffee-mill they used a pestle and mortar. I prefer the pestle and mortar myself, because it preserves the aroma, but perhaps that's my imagination.

Desi Arnaz, the television star, was born Desiderio Alberto Arnaz y de Acha in Santiago de Cuba in 1917. His family was wealthy and politically powerful. In his autobiography, Arnaz recalled his childhood.

My father, besides being the mayor, had three farms. On one of them he raised cattle. Another was a dairy farm. He was the first man to build a pasteurization plant in our province and also the first to use refrigerated trucks to deliver the milk. The third farm was used for poultry and pig raising and had a slaughterhouse where meat, sausages and all other products of this kind were processed and sold.

During school vacations there was always work for me at one of the farms. My father felt that if I wanted new oars for the boat or a motor overhaul or whatever, I should earn the money to pay for it. I didn't mind; it was fun.

I would get up at dawn with the other hands to start the day's chores. Every morning we had a contest to see who could fill a bucket with milk the quickest. Each of us would put up five cents and the one who could fill the bucket first would take the pot. I became pretty good at milking cows.

Digna Olga-Blanco grew up in Cuba during the 1940s. Today she has her own business designing wedding gowns in a suburb of Boston.

I was born in Santa Lucía, a beautiful city on the ocean. It's like Hawaii, with beautiful fruits—pears, and grapes, and coconuts. My father had a store that sold everything, including cloth. My mother would take a piece of that fabric and make a dress for me. And watching her sewing, I learned to sew by the time I was ten years old. I loved to sew and was always creating and producing—always. I made shirts for my brothers.

My aunt was a very special person in my life. I really loved her a lot. I remember at Christmas she would make something like a velvet dress, she would copy things from American magazines. That was when my love affair with the United States began. I would say, "Oh, I want to go to the United States." That was my dream.

At the age of 14, I went to Havana, to a school for design. After only one year I graduated with honors.... My teachers asked me, "Did somebody teach you at home?" I was so eager to learn.

The next year this very rich lady hired me.... She was a concert pianist, and she would get small models of dresses from designers from Europe. She brought them back and I would have to enlarge them into a gown. She was a tall, very good-looking lady, French and Cuban. Her father was Ernesto Lecuona, Cuba's most famous composer. He wrote "Granada."

I could actually write a book about the year I spent with that lady. She was very splendid. She used to tell her chauffeur,

The Havana harbor in the early 20th century. The city, on the northern coast of the island, was founded by the Spanish in 1514. It soon became a base for Spanish expeditions to North and South America. Today, it remains Cuba's busiest port.

13

José Martí

The father of Cuban independence, José Martí was born in Havana in 1853. His Spanish-born father was a first sergeant in the Spanish Royal Artillery. Young Martí came of age after Cuban patriots started the Ten Years' War in 1868. Though José was only a teenager, his public support for the independence fighters caused the Spanish authorities to arrest him. In 1871, he was exiled to Spain.

While there, Martí graduated from college. He then began a career as a journalist, teacher, and poet in Mexico and Guatemala. Embarking for Cuba in 1878, he wrote a letter to a friend that summed up his feelings: "Shall I tell you...that I carry my unhappy people in my head, and that it seems to me that their liberty will some day depend upon one breath of mine?... They think that I am returning to my country.... I no longer have a country—until I conquer it." Soon after Martí's arrival, he was arrested and exiled once more. He would not return to Cuba until the year of his death.

Martí settled in New York City, where he devoted himself to organizing a new struggle for Cuban independence. At the same time, he continued his writing. For a short time, he published a magazine for children.

In 1891, Martí made his first trip to Florida, where he met with Cuban cigar workers in Tampa and Key West. He started to organize them into a political party that would work for independence. The following year, the Cuban Revolutionary Party was established with Martí as its head.

By 1895, Martí had raised enough funds from Cubans in the United States to supply a revolutionary army. The date of the invasion was smuggled to Martí's allies in Cuba inside a cigar. On April 11, Martí and his forces landed on the island. Eight days later, he was killed in the fighting. He was mourned throughout Cuban communities in both countries. Although he did not see his goals fulfilled, the rebellion he started would eventually win Cuba its independence.

Bernardo, "I want my girls to go to a show, or a club." I had my own private room, and whenever I needed something, she would say, "Make a list, and Bernardo will take you to the finest stores in Havana." I would ride in the back seat like a princess.

But you know, I never cared for money. I told my mother, "She has money, mama, but she's crazy."

The poet Pablo Medina was born in Havana in 1948 and came to the United States when he was 12 years old. He wrote about the splendors of Havana in his memoir Exiled Memories: A Cuban Childhood.

The Havana of my childhood is the most beautiful city I have known.... The place I loved to go most on Sunday afternoons was the Malecón, a wide boulevard that rounded the bay from Almendares to the statue of Antonio Maceo, the hero of the War of Independence. The waves crashed against the quay that kept the sea from eating away at the pavement, sending huge explosions of spray over the wall and onto the sidewalk. Groups of boys played tag with the water, walking until a wave crashed, then running from the spray, sometimes right into the street and the oncoming traffic, to avoid getting drenched.

Across the street where only the mist reached, the boulevard was lined with stalls selling foods and drinks of all kinds: *fritas* [fritters], *papas rellenas* [stuffed potatoes], *empanadas* [meat or guava pastries], *pasteles* [pastries], *pan con lechón* [pork sandwich], *guarapo* [sugarcane juice], papaya juice, mango juice, and the oranges peeled and cut the way you wanted. Up and down the sidewalk, *cafeteros* [coffee-vendors] with their thermoses full of black, strong coffee intoned their cry: *Café, un kilo, un kilo café* [one-cent coffee]. There were also *maniceros* [peanut vendors] carrying large tin cans loaded with peanut cones: *Maní, manicero aquí, cucuruchos de maní* [peanuts, peanuts here, paper cones of peanuts].

In this Havana orchestra around 1915, the boy at the center of the front row is Mario Bauza, who came to the United States in the 1920s. He was a major influence on both Cuban and American jazz.

At the intersections, photographers dressed in dark, wrinkled suits took pictures of whole families out for a Sunday stroll, which they developed in cans hanging under their tripods. And everywhere there were children playing, chasing each other, darting in and out through groups of passersby, daring each other to do this and that, the mothers chastising, threatening, the fathers walking imperturbably on in their white *guayaberas* [shirts].

On the horizon, the shipping lanes provided a parade of vessels that filled a boy's head with seafaring fantasies: cargo ships, fishing trawlers, sailing schooners, warships, and always the cruise ships that slowly made their way in the bay and spewed their cargo of *americanos* in for a week of leisure.

Ruth Behar, an anthropologist and writer, came to the United States with her family in 1962, when she was a child. She wrote about her parents' different Jewish backgrounds. Her father's family came from Turkey; her mother's from Poland.

It was in Havana that my mother met my father. Their relationship was a cross-cultural encounter, for my father was a *turco* who came from a traditional Turkish Sephardic background, in which Ladino, the old Spanish of the expelled Jews, was still spoken at home. He had grown up street-smart near the docks of Havana, and, though a first-generation Cuban like my mother, his black hair and *habanero* [Havana gentleman] style allowed him to pass more easily as a Cuban. His father was a peddler who worked only half the day and spent the afternoons playing dominoes with his buddies. If my mother's family were doing only moderately well, my father's family were barely making it. Some time in the late 1930s, when my father's family had gone hungry for several days, my grandfather brought home an excellent cut of beef. It had been given to him by one of his clients, and he presented it with enormous satisfaction to my grandmother. She refused to accept it because it wasn't kosher meat. My grandfather insisted she take it, saying it was a gift and that they were too hungry to be choosy. My grandmother kept refusing. My grandfather kept insisting. Finally, my grandmother took the meat from him. Holding it in her determined hands, she lifted the package high above her head and flung it out the window. The argument that ensued must have been momentous because the story about the beef that ended up in the street has never been forgotten in my father's family.

My father has often claimed that it was my mother who taught him to eat the prohibited foods that his mother had so vehemently kept out of her house. Not that my mother allowed unkosher meat in her house, either. At home she translated recipes from her Cuban cookbook, *Cocina Criolla*, itself a creole culinary mix, making kosher *tamales* and kosher *caldo gallego* [Galician soup] by substituting chicken and Hebrew National beef fry for the pork that was supposed to be in these dishes.

This shrine to a saint is found in one of Cuba's many Catholic churches. Decorated with jewelry and handicrafts, it reflects the intense religious devotion that is a traditional part of Catholicism.

The man at right sells tickets in the Cuban national lottery around 1915. Lotteries were popular among poorer Cubans, who saw them as the only way of gaining wealth.

Public marketplaces, traditionally a part of every Cuban community, offer a wide variety of goods. This woman sells pet birds.

Rosa Vazquez was born in the city of Santa Clara, in Las Villas Province, in 1954. She described what it was like to grow up as a member of a large family in a small Cuban town.

I grew up in a little town next to Santa Clara called Ranchuelo.... As a child, I felt happy, and very sheltered, and very loved. Because it was a small town, everybody knew me. On my mother's side, there were nine children; on my father's side there were five children. So I have an immense extended family, and I had a lot of first cousins and second cousins. I used to spend weekends at my maternal grandmother's and grandfather's house, which was in another little town, much more rural. That grandfather came from Spain. *Asturiano*—he was from Asturias. My grandmother also was the daughter of Asturianos.

My grandpa was brought from Spain by his older brother José who was already making some money in Cuba. My grandfather, Manolo, also started making money with his brother. Manolo and José married two sisters, two Cuban-born daughters of Spaniards. Manolo had nine kids, José had six. And they lived in one house, with a common kitchen, a cook, and some maids, to take care of all of these kids. This family is still—I call them uncles and aunts, my second cousins. A very big, happy family. I have good memories.

The majority of Cubans had a low standard of living, even in the 1950s, when this photo was taken. For children, there was no place to play except the streets. Shoes were an expense that few could afford.

Margarita Sainz de la Peña Gagliardi lived in Cuba until she was seven years old. She later recalled visits to her grandparents' ranch in the countryside.

I was born in Camagüey, Cuba, July 1, 1955. Our family was somewhat prominent in Cuba. My maternal grandparents were ranchers and had orange groves as well as sugar cane fields. My maternal grandparents' home was out in the country, in a small town called La Gloria, which was, interestingly, settled by Americans. So my parents actually grew up speaking English and having American friends. Which was somewhat unusual.

My grandmother's house I remember like I was just there yesterday. It was a big old wooden structure. It had a veranda on all three sides, papaya trees in the back, and it was just a lovely, lovely place.

I think one of my most pleasant experiences was when people would come in with little cubes of sugar cane, straight from the fields. We would sit on my grandmother's back steps and chew on them. You suck all the sugar and sweetness out of them. That was a special treat for us, when they'd come in from the fields with the sugar cane.

Hamlet Arias was born in Cuba in 1973 and left there when he was eight years old. He now lives in New York City, where he told an interviewer about his family's history.

As the story goes, my grandmother was a washerwoman in Havana when she was young. And this young Spanish officer brought his uniform to her to be washed.

Well he kept bringing his uniform, and she was a beautiful young woman. So he became interested in her in a romantic way. But she told him, "I'm not going to be a little fling for you," you know, like a one-night stand. She said, "If you love me, then you will have to marry me and buy me a house and provide for any children we have."

So that's what he did. And they had a big house and ten children. Some Spanish women were always coming to visit my grandfather, and they started to gossip. They couldn't believe he was married to this dark-skinned Cuban woman. So you know what my grandmother did? She put their marriage certificate on the door of the house! That stopped all the talk....

When my mother became pregnant, she started to read Shakespeare's plays. And by the time I appeared, she had read all of them. The doctor asked her what my name would be, and she just chose her favorite character—Hamlet. My niece is named Juliet. And I plan to keep up the tradition, when I get married and have children....

My full name is Hamlet Arias Monzón. When I came here and became a citizen, they took out the Monzón, so now I'm Hamlet Arias. That's what it says on my social security card.

My childhood was like spun sugar. It was quite literally rosy from the moment you woke up to the moment you went to sleep. On the one hand, there was very little pressure on a girl growing up in Havana society, at least before the age of thirteen. If you did not do well in school, you were likely to be told, "Oh, don't worry, my darling, you'll marry a fine man and it won't make any difference anyway." And besides, there were so many activities for us, so many things on offer in our beautiful, beautiful Havana that were just guaranteed to delight even the most morose child.

—Teresita de Blank, the daughter of sugar planters who left Cuba right after the revolution

Sugarcane cutters in Cuba in the early 20th century. From the 1890s until the 1960s, nearly all of the harvest was exported to the United States. When the U.S. government halted trade with Cuba, the island's economy suffered.

THE REVOLUTION

When Fidel Castro came to power in 1959, most Cubans hoped he would bring greater prosperity and social equality to the country. Here, a man shows Castro a child wearing a false beard that imitates Castro's.

Fidel Castro's victory was particularly vivid for Tamahra Calzadilla because her father had been an official in the Batista government.

I remember Castro coming into power.... It was quite scary. I remember father coming in early, at dawn, and we all woke up, and he just told my mother, "I'm leaving. I'm going to pack some of my things and I am leaving. I have to go," and he said he would be taking a plane at 4 o'clock in the morning and gave my mother instructions to take us at 6 o'clock in the morning, the chauffeur would come to pick us up, and we went to a farm to hide.

My father belonged to the Batista government and he had to leave in exile before he was shot [by] Castro's people.... I remember leaving at 6 o'clock that morning. The chauffeur came to pick us up, we went to the farm, and we just took with us what we had on and whatever jewelry we had on. In the afternoon my aunt came to pick up our clothes at our house and everything was stolen. Everything including furniture and clothing and jewelry, whatever was left in that house was stolen by the people that were for Castro. Those people with the knowledge that my father was part of the Batista government, of course, they hated him. And Castro was looking for my father and a lot of other Batista people. It was just very terrifying. I remember we didn't have anything to wear, I remember we were at the farm and I had to wear the owner's of the farm, his underwear, and that's all I had for clothing with the exception of what I had brought with me. And after about a month we came back into Havana and stayed in hiding in my aunt's house in Havana. And we were children. I have three sisters, three older sisters, and my two older sisters, of course, knew what was going on, but the third one and myself, we didn't know and we were children. We weren't allowed to go out in the street to play because they were looking for us. My mother was with us at all times.

The poet Pablo Medina described the heady days after the fall of Batista.

5 A.M., January 1, 1959, my father rushed into my grandmother's bedroom where I had stayed the night. At first, still in the grip of dreams, I saw him through a haze, his face flushed, eyes round and open. He waved his arms and his mouth was moving, but I couldn't at that instant between sleep and wakedom, make out what he was saying. In a few seconds, his words had broken through

This Castro doll was sold by street vendors as a toy in the early years of his regime.

my slumber. "¡Cayó Batista!" "Batista fell!"

I jumped out of bed and rushed out to the backyard.... The whole family was cheering and dancing, giving thanks to God that the tyrant had, at long last, been deposed. It was a day of rejoicing, of reveling in a collective hope shared by most that things would be good now, that peace had come and corruption had been eradicated. Such feelings I have never since experienced: a bit like drunkenness, yet lighter than that and clearer, like the warm air of that beautiful day, shared by all.

The craziness spilled over onto the following week and no one bothered to go to work. The whole city was engulfed in the celebration. Patriotic banners appeared everywhere. People smiled. At times one would hear a shout coming from a car driving by or from a stranger across the street: "*¡Viva Fidel! ¡Viva Cuba Libre!*" Throughout the week we awaited the arrival of the rebels into the capital....

Fidel Castro arrived in Havana on January 8 at the head of a column of *barbudos*, or bearded ones. With him were el Che [Che Guevara, an Argentinian revolutionary leader who aided Castro in his revolution], his brother Raúl, Camilo Cienfuegos, and all the mythic figures who had fought in the Sierra Maestra. For a boy like myself, whose dreams fed on the feats of warriors struggling against evil, the appearance of the triumphant bearded ones on the streets of my city was the ultimate confirmation that heroes existed beyond the pages of adventure novels.

The whole city turned out to greet them. Women and children crowded round to kiss, to touch, to embrace them.

Trucks carried people from the countryside into Havana to celebrate Castro's victory. His rebellion was called the 26th of July Movement, after the date in 1953 when Castro led an unsuccessful attack on an army barracks. Captured and exiled, he returned in 1956.

Women joined Castro's rebel band, which hid in the Sierra Maestra after Castro landed on the island in 1956. These young women listen to one of Castro's victory speeches in 1959.

Seeing a rebel on the street was enough to make the heart jump, for they were viewed with an awe bordering on the reverence reserved for saints. These were, after all, our young liberators and they looked the part. Their long hair tied in pony tails, their black berets, their olive green uniforms, and their gun belts were to set the style for many a "revolutionary" of the future. Around their necks hung rosaries, religious medals, scapulae, and other mementos given to them by thankful citizens on their march to Havana.

A 16-year-old Cuban refugee, who gave his name as Jorge to interviewer Janet Bode in in the 1980s, described his early years in Castro's Cuba.

In Cuba, the government controls your life. Everything is rationed. Each family has a little booklet called a "libreta" with coupons in it. You want to buy a pair of pants? You can't just run over to K-Mart or Macy's or some shopping center. In Cuba, each family is assigned a special week to shop for clothes, say, May 21 to May 28, and K-Marts don't exist. You're supposed to go those days to get what the coupons say, maybe one skirt or one shirt. You get one pair of shoes for one year. Even underwear is rationed, three pairs for each person for one year. The same thing with toys.

Depending on how many people live in your house, you have a certain number of coupons for food, too. Your family is assigned to go to one particular store; that is the only one that accepts our coupons. When I am in Cuba my favorite food is rice and beans and roast pork. But it is hard to find pork. Any meat is hard to find. I don't even know there are such things as shrimp, clams, and lobsters, and Cuba is an island surrounded by shellfish. I only learned about these things once I come here.

Amaury Almaguer left Cuba in 1980. Today a successful businessman in New Orleans, he described his youth in Castro's Cuba.

I was born in Holguín, Oriente Province, Cuba. Mother was a homemaker, and Father was a Cuban soldier. My sister and I attended local schools. I took pleasure in writing, and while a student, my account of a local sports event appeared in the town newspaper. Life in Cuba was repressive, and if you rejected concepts imposed by the government you were imprisoned. In company with four other youths, I was accused of sabotage for writing messages—conflicting with communistic beliefs—on street walls. Three youths died; two were apprehended. I was sentenced to five years in a penal institution. Although I was sixteen years old and prosecuted as an adult, no one tried to secure my release, because I [had] committed a political crime. Actually, Father's behavior suggested that in attacking the Cuban revolution I assaulted him personally. On 4 April 1972 I arrived at Boniato, a prison in Santiago de Cuba near the city of Guantánamo. Prisoners had the option to enter a rehabilitation program that included work in construction or in sugarcane fields and a reduced sentence, or serve the required period. The latter was severe, in view of the fact that these prisoners received less food, limited medical attention, and had no visitation rights. I chose the harsher sentence. However, if offered the selection today I would again elect prison, with its accompanying physical pain, because my personality evolved from association with inmates who possessed high ideals. I entered prison at 16 and departed at 20 with a tenacious disposition.

William Wieland, Cuban desk officer at the U.S. State Department, explained why the United States supported Batista:

I know Batista is considered by many as a son of a bitch...but American interests come first.... At least he is our son of a bitch, he is not playing ball with the Communists.... On the other hand, Fidel Castro is surrounded by commies.

Facing certain defeat, dictator Fulgencio Batista fled Cuba late in 1958. Crowds like this one at Cienfuegos greeted the victorious Fidel Castro (top center) as he led his forces toward Havana.

A kindergarten class, taught by Mary B. Espinosa, in Sancti Spíritus, Cuba, in 1954. Few families could afford to give their children this kind of education during Batista's regime. Castro closed all private and religious schools after he came to power.

Members of Cuba's wealthy and privileged elite—such as these people eating lunch at a private club in Havana in 1955—were among those who left the island after Castro seized their businesses and ranches.

THE DECISION TO LEAVE

Robert de Castro came to the United States from Cuba in 1943. Today a successful businessman, he remembered that it was the American dream of opportunity that attracted him to the United States.

A man who repaired the artesian well on our farm frequently spoke of economic opportunities available in the United States. My father, who had visited the United States, also encouraged me to migrate and repeatedly told me, "That's the land of opportunity—go over there and seek your fortune. If it doesn't work out, then you come back."

Noemi de Diaz came to the United States in 1955 after earning a doctorate in law and attending a Presbyterian seminary in Matanzas. When she learned that the church in Cuba allowed women to serve as ministers only if they remained unmarried, she thought of working elsewhere.

Through one of my professors at the seminary, I learned of the need for Christian workers within the Spanish-speaking community in New York City. Because of my background in law, I became especially interested in the possibilities of working for greater social justice and better opportunities for this population, as well as trying to live the Good News of Christ in the midst of human suffering.

Another reason was that at the seminary we needed English, and I decided that one of my goals was to learn the language because I would like to read theological books in English. And my husband was working in the merchant marine, traveling back and forth between Cuba and New York, and he said, "In my point of view, it is the same if you live in Havana or in New York, because I have been in both places." My son was also by that time a senior in high school, and he also wanted to come to the United States.

Elsa Lake was born and raised in Cuba, the daughter of a teacher and a doctor. After graduating from the University of Havana with a law degree, Elsa worked in the Cuban government. She soon became disenchanted with the regime of Fidel Castro and fled to this country in 1960, settling in New Jersey. She explained why she wanted to leave.

I felt it was a matter of surviving. Get out of the country or be killed.

When the revolution started, it was not clear what ideas Castro had and what he intended to do with the government. It was much later that the true situation of communism came about.... I had finished law school and gotten a job with the department dealing with taxes. Working for an office of the government, I was being forced to do things that I didn't like, and of course I flatly refused. I became more open in... verbalizing how much I disliked communism. It got to the point when I knew that they would threaten my life and that I was headed toward a dead end. I had to leave or I didn't know what was going to happen to me.

Ramon Fernandez came to the United States in 1961. He described his father's decision to leave.

And then, of course, when Castro took over, everything was different. They began taking over certain companies—big companies and socializing them. You could see the trend. And my father used to argue with some folks about the way communism worked when it came into a country and the first things they started doing. Right away he started smelling a rat. One day there was a big hassle in the Catholic school. The guys came in with guns and started threatening the nuns. Things like that. A couple of priests got beaten up. They were trying to stop all kinds of religion. So my father decided it was time to leave the country.

Irma de Leon was a judge at the time of the Castro revolution.

The Revolution brought an abrupt change to my life. Everything that I had been taught and stood for changed. Castro appeared on television and reported, "Last night we passed a law and everybody who doesn't agree with it will be put into prison." I knew then I would have to leave or they would kill me. In May 1962 I made a decision to leave Cuba.

As a boy, Rodolfo de León lived in the coastal town of Santa Lucía. He recalled the day in the early 1960s when his family decided to leave Cuba.

We were at the beach, and my father called us. We waited for him at the entrance of Santa Lucía. We waited a lot that day, and he didn't come. Finally, he came with the news that his business had been confiscated. They had offered him the job of administering it. He refused. Immediately he brought the lawyer with him to make up papers and passports for us to leave.

From then on everything was downhill. I felt there was something bad going on, that we were going to leave the country. I didn't know what the hell that *meant*! I didn't know. I didn't know what that meant that I was going to go somewhere else; I didn't have any idea of sociological orders, economic ideas, whatever. I wasn't aware of a lot of things.

I remember crying when he told us that. I was really upset.

As Others Saw Them

I approached the outskirts of the city [Havana] in almost ideal conditions, with Jerry [a guide] at my elbow explaining what areas we were traversing. As I twisted my head excitedly from side to side, I expected to see the kind of Hispanic city with which I had become so familiar during my protracted residences in Spain, Mexico, and South Texas.

What a shock! "My God! This city needs ten million dollars' worth of white paint!" for the houses and business places in that part of town were so decrepit in appearance that anyone who lived in cities would have to protest. It was not one house or building that was devoid of paint; it was entire streets, almost whole districts; proof that a beautiful city was wearing away was inescapable.

My next shock came when we left what had been essentially a business district and entered upon a chain of streets containing private houses with lawns, but since none of the householders had access to mowers, the grass grew wild, almost obscuring the residences behind. No family with even a glimmer of pride would want to live in such a setting; every inclination would be to get out and chop down that offending grass, but when there were no aids to help, the householders obviously said, "To hell with it."

—Novelist James Michener, who visited Cuba for six days in 1988, while doing research for a book.

After the United States withdrew recognition of Castro's government, it halted trade with Cuba. Other non-communist nations joined the trade embargo. As a result, new automobiles and new parts for old ones became scarce. By 1970, when this photo was taken, the effort to coax old cars back into life was a familiar sight on Cuban streets.

23

Workers construct public housing in Havana in 1976. Economic aid from the Soviet Union for such projects helped Castro's government survive.

Roberto Ortiz left Cuba for the United States in 1962. It was the scarcity of food and other goods that impelled him to leave.

Things started to get tough.... You could not get food. Food is getting very scarce. Restaurants started closing and stores closing, and the black market [selling food at illegally high prices] started very bad. When you go and see a relative and they don't have food to put on the table, this is bad! When you walk in there, and you see they don't want to eat because you are in there, and they are waiting for you to leave, to eat. And when you got to do the same thing at home—I couldn't live with it, and decided to leave from a combination of all these things.

David Sagarra, an artist, recalled that the revolution made it difficult for him to paint what he wished.

As a painter I would have had to join the official painters' association in order to obtain paints, brushes, and oils to produce canvasses and paintings. When you eliminate the possibility for an individual to go to the corner and buy a tube of paint, you are really depriving him of freely painting whatever he wants. The government did specify quite clearly that the subject matter was to be limited to whatever did not contradict the revolution.

Mike Yip, today the manager and part-owner of a Cuban-Chinese restaurant in New York, explained why he left Cuba in 1969.

I was only four or five years old when the Revolution started. It affected a lot of my family in Cuba, because at that time my father had a restaurant, businesses. And when Castro took over, with the revolution, he took over everybody's businesses. Everything over there belongs to the government, not to you. You're not the owner of anything. At the beginning, things weren't so bad, but later everything began to get worse....

In Cuba, from age 15 to 26 you have to serve in the military. Once you reach the age of 15, they won't let you leave. So in 1969, I was 14 years old and decided to leave. I came by myself, first to get away from the military draft, and also to find out what it was like here. My mother, my sister, and my father stayed behind in Cuba. Later, I was able to bring them over too.

A man named Danilo escaped from Cuba in 1979. On arrival, he told an interviewer why he decided to leave.

I left because the salary I made in Cuba was not enough to support my wife and son. Because there is so much hunger I had to go fishing and sell what I caught to buy rice, even though this kind of thing is prohibited. I had to buy beans and other food on the black market. And you know what happens to you when they catch you doing that—you are put in jail. I used to carry a shopping bag with me to be able to buy what I needed whenever I happened to find it. I was lucky they never stopped me, but you are afraid all the time. I planned that if they ever caught me I would say that a friend had given me these things. The government, however, has its own system, too. They check to see if the rice or whatever you have is the same as your friend's. You just have to take the chance, anyway.

There is much repression of all kinds in Cuba. Every day when you are at the bus stop they ask for your ID. If you walk with a package they ask to see what is inside. If they notice a few of you on a corner, they tell you, "Go on. Scram."

The U.S.-led trade embargo hurt the Cuban economy badly. These people wait in line to buy food at a bodega, or grocery store. Such hardships caused many more Cubans to attempt to flee the country after the 1960s than before.

Refugees display the Cuban flag on a small boat headed for the United States.

CHAPTER TWO

COMING TO THE UNITED STATES

The ties between Cuba and Florida—where nearly 700,000 Cuban Americans live today—are almost five centuries old. The first Spanish explorers arrived in Florida in 1513, claiming it for Spain but departing soon afterward. In 1538, the king of Spain appointed Hernando de Soto as governor of Cuba, instructing him to explore Florida further. The next year, de Soto left Havana with nine ships carrying more than 500 men and 200 horses. His expedition roamed through what is now the southeastern United States, from North Carolina to Arkansas.

In 1564, French Protestants seeking a refuge from religious persecution established a settlement at what is now Jacksonville, Florida. The Spaniards could not tolerate this threat to their hold on Florida, especially by "heretics" who were not Roman Catholic. Pedro Menéndez de Avilés arrived the next year with a force of 1,500 soldiers, who destroyed the French settlement. That same year, 1565, Menéndez founded what is today the oldest city in the United States—St. Augustine, Florida.

For almost a century and a half, St. Augustine remained the only Spanish foothold on the Atlantic

coast of North America. Another Spanish settlement was founded at Pensacola, on the west coast of Florida, in 1696. The Spanish seldom ventured far inland, for the Native Americans of Florida proved to be considerably fiercer in defending themselves than the natives of Cuba had been.

In 1819, Spain sold Florida to the United States for $5 million. It was not long before Cubans began to migrate to the United States. Among the earliest were merchants who established import-export businesses in New York and Philadelphia.

Others were political exiles. One of them was Father Félix Varela, a Catholic priest who had been named a Cuban delegate to the Spanish Cortes in 1821. Forced to flee Spain because of his radical political ideas, Varela arrived in New York City in December 1823. From then until his death in 1853, he remained in exile in the United States, publishing pamphlets and newspapers advocating Cuban independence.

Varela was the first of a long line of Cubans who found refuge from political oppression in the United States. During the Ten Years' War of 1868-78, several thousand Cubans fled north. By the mid-1870s, Cubans lived in New York City, Philadelphia,

New Orleans, Boston, and Key West, Florida.

In the late 1860s and 1870s, some Cuban cigar manufacturers established factories in the United States to avoid tariffs and Spanish trade regulations on their goods. In the next few decades, these factories provided employment for Cuban immigrants. Key West and Ybor City (today part of Tampa) in Florida became thriving centers of Cuban American life. In 1876, Carlos Manuel de Céspedes, the son of a Cuban veteran of the Ten Years' War, was elected mayor of Key West.

Workers commonly traveled from Cuba to Florida or New York City, took jobs for a time, and then returned home. A U.S. congressional committee estimated in 1892 that between 50,000 and 100,000 people traveled between Cuba and the United States in a year. That was far more than the number of people who settled permanently.

Even after Cuba won its independence, the United States remained a haven for Cubans fleeing political persecution. After 1952, when Fulgencio Batista returned to power, his repressive policies caused a steady increase in the number of Cuban immigrants. About 80,000 arrived during Batista's regime, which ended on January 1, 1959.

Those numbers, however, were insignificant compared to the tide of refugees who have fled the government of Fidel Castro since 1959. The first wave of refugees was known as the "golden exiles." Many were relatively wealthy people whose property had been confiscated by Castro's communist government. Before commercial air flights between the two countries were suspended in October 1962, about 200,000 Cubans arrived through the airports of Miami and New York.

About 14,000 of them were unaccompanied children, rushed out of Cuba as part of a program called Operation Pedro Pan (Peter Pan). Catholic Church groups and others encouraged the idea that these children were in danger of being sent to the Soviet Union for communist indoctrination. After they arrived in the United States, some of these children were given assistance to obtain visas for their parents. However, as many as half of them may never have been reunited with their families.

From 1962 to 1965, refugees continued to leave the island by booking airplane flights to third countries, such as Mexico and Spain. About 50,000 of them then headed for the United States.

In September 1965, Castro announced that Cubans with relatives living in the United States could leave on boats through the small port of Camarioca on the northern coast. A panic ensued as thousands of Cubans headed for

Camarioca. Relatives in Florida sent boats to help them escape, but many of the craft were not seaworthy, and their passengers drowned.

As a result, in December 1965 the governments of the United States and Cuba signed a "memorandum of understanding" reestablishing air flights between Miami and Varadero, Cuba. During the next eight years—the time of the "Freedom Flights"—about 300,000 more Cubans took this route to the United States.

In April 1973, the Cuban government again discontinued the direct flights. For the next seven years, the flow of immigration slowed drastically. Castro's government allowed about 14,000 political prisoners and their families to leave the island between October 1978 and April 1980.

In December 1978, Castro announced that he would permit Cubans living in the United States to return for one-week visits with family members in Cuba. Castro hoped to show that his govern-

Journalists leave Cuba during Fulgencio Batista's repressive regime in the 1950s. Later, when Fidel Castro came to power, he, too, severely restricted freedom of the press.

ment was secure enough to allow such visits. The relatives from the United States also brought gifts and money that pumped about $100 million into Cuba's weak economy. However, the move backfired; the visitors' prosperity drew a sharp contrast between life in the United States and life in communist Cuba. Increasingly, lower-class Cubans— those who were supposed to have benefited most from Castro's policies— began to seek ways to emigrate.

In April 1980, a group of Cubans forced their way into the Peruvian embassy in Havana, asking for political asylum. When the Cuban government allowed them to leave the island, more than 10,000 people applied at the embassy for exit visas. Embarrassed, Castro announced that he would open the port of Mariel to any Cubans who wanted to go directly to the United States. U.S. President Jimmy Carter declared that the United States would "provide an open heart and open arms for the tens of thousands of refugees seeking freedom from communist domination."

Once again, Cuban Americans responded by launching a flotilla of fishing boats, ferries, outboard motorboats, and yachts to bring the new refugees from Mariel. U.S. Highway 1, which links Miami with Key West, was choked with automobiles towing boats to the jumping-off point for the Mariel boatlift. It turned out to be an enormous undertaking. In a little more than five months, about 125,000 Cubans were brought to the United States.

Enraged by this demonstration of his unpopularity, Castro forced onto the boats thousands of people whom he regarded as "undesirables." These included not only prisoners from jail but also patients from mental hospitals, homosexuals, and people with physical handicaps.

This policy tarred all "Marielitos" (those who came to the United States via the Mariel boatlift) as potential criminals. The U.S. government herded about 22,000 of the refugees into temporary shelters, trying to determine which ones really were criminals. Most of the Marielitos who had been in jail in Cuba turned out to have been sentenced for political activities or minor crimes, and they were released. Eventually, about 3,700 others were sent to federal prisons, where they were held for the next seven years without trials or legal hearings.

In 1987, Castro offered to resume air flights between his country and the United States. Before agreeing, the U.S. government demanded that Castro accept the return of the Marielitos in U.S. prisons. When the prisoners heard of this, they staged protest riots, claiming that to be sent back to Cuba meant certain death. A U.S. district court judge ordered that all prisoners should receive the right to plead their cases in court. Fewer than a thousand were declared "excludable aliens" and returned to Cuba.

Each year from 1988 through 1993, between 3,000 and 4,000 Cubans arrived in the United States via regular air flights. However, many who could not obtain visas or purchase plane tickets made the decision to try to reach the United States by sea. Called *balseros*, or "rafters," such people thought that they could make the 90-mile trip between Cuba and Key West on rafts thrown together from boards and inner tubes. U.S. Coast Guard ships frequently plucked the *balseros* from the sea and took them to Florida. But others perished, for storms and currents made the crossing hazardous.

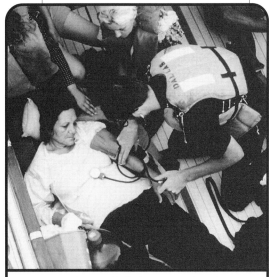

Many people were killed or injured in desperate attempts to cross the Straits of Florida to the United States. The woman shown here is being treated by medical personnel from a U.S. Coast Guard vessel.

Some who completed the journey reported that they had spent more than two weeks at sea, though they carried food and water for only a few days. No one can say how many *balseros* lost their lives trying to reach land.

In the summer of 1994, another crisis brought the issue of Cuban *balseros* into the headlines. Since 1991, when the Soviet Union dissolved, Cuba's economy had suffered from the loss of aid from its former communist ally. High unemployment and food shortages caused protest demonstrations against the Castro regime. In August 1994, Castro declared that he would no longer prevent Cubans from trying to leave the island by sea. Within a month, tens of thousands of *balseros* tried to make the dangerous trip.

Alarmed by this sudden influx of refugees, U.S. President Bill Clinton abruptly changed the government's policy of carrying them to Florida. Instead, he ordered that all *balseros* taken on board U.S. ships be brought to the U.S. naval base at Guantánamo Bay, Cuba.

In May 1995, the Clinton administration agreed to admit them into the United States.

At the same time, however, the United States announced that it had reached an agreement in secret negotiations with the Cuban government. Because both governments wished to prevent unsafe departures from the island, the United States agreed that in the future, Cubans leaving in boats for the United States would be taken back to Cuba. This reversed a 35-year-long policy of welcoming the *balseros*, and it angered many in the Cuban American community.

Between 1960 and 1995 more than 1 million Cubans have arrived in the United States— almost 10 percent of the island's population. Except for the mass emigration from Ireland in the 19th century, never before has that high a percentage of another nation's people arrived in the United States in so short a time.

In the early 1960s, Castro permitted Cubans to leave the country as long as they left their money and property behind. Here, a U.S. Customs official in Cuba examines the papers of refugees boarding a ship for the United States.

In 1980 Cuban exiles in Miami show support for Cubans who had taken refuge inside the Peruvian embassy in Havana. The embassy incident led to the Mariel boatlift, in which Cubans in the United States helped about 125,000 people cross the Straits of Florida in a flotilla of small boats.

LEAVING HOME

Gustavo Pérez Firmat, a writer and professor at Duke University, describes leaving home on October 24, 1960, when he was a boy of 11.

That morning Nena, my mother, woke us up earlier than usual. It was a school day, but we weren't going to school. In the hallway outside my bedroom the queue of suitcases stretched all the way to the front door. For several years I had been coming to the States once or twice a year, always taking the *City of Havana*, the overnight ferry to Key West. From there we would drive or take a train to Crowley, Louisiana, the rice capital of America, where my father did business.... As usual, I got up that morning looking forward to sleeping aboard the ship and waking up the next day to the sight of the sandbars ranged along the Keys like pillows.

We arrived at the pier a couple of hours before the ferry was scheduled to sail. I had been here many times before, since my father's food wholesaling business, which we always called *el almacén*, was only a few blocks away. (An *almacén*, literally, is a storehouse, but in Cuba the term referred primarily to food wholesalers and distributors; *almacén* was short for *almacén de víveres*, a storehouse of eatables.) This morning my aunt Cuca drove us to the dock, where my father joined us. After our suitcases were opened and checked, some question arose about his passport. The ferry's departure was delayed for an hour. Finally, the problem was straightened out and sometime in the early afternoon the *City of Havana* began to inch away from the pier. My aunt waved good-bye. We waved back. Pepe [my brother] and I clutched the small metal safes with the money that we had saved to spend on our next trip to the States.

Between 1960 and 1962, more than 14,000 Cuban children were sent to the United States as part of the Pedro Pan Program. Through this program, Catholic social agencies helped children gain entrance to the United States. Then the children would enable their parents to gain admittance through programs that sought to unify families.

Flora González Mandri, today a professor of literature at Emerson College, was one of those children. Born in 1948 in Havana, she grew up in Camagüey. In January 1962, she was a 12-year-old girl leaving her parents and traveling to the United States with her sister Alicia. The two sisters went to live in Ukiah, California, and were reunited with their parents in Miami only in June 1963.

We were all at the airport inside a huge room with glass walls, my sister and I in an aquarium with a lot of strangers and our parents on the other side of the glass; especially Mami who was crying, trying to give us final instructions, moving her lips with a voice that transmitted no sound. And I...couldn't read the words from her lips. Not a sound! All that came through was the anguish in her face, wrinkling up her forehead, telling me in sign language not to hide anything, not to keep my watch and my rings in my pockets like everybody else so that they wouldn't be confiscated. And my sister and I, like fools, didn't hide anything and naturally they took everything away from us. Including that ring with an enormous aquamarine that my aunt Estrella had given me just before I left Camagüey, the one that used to make me feel so grown up. They did it just to bother us because the jewelry was returned to the family members who stayed behind....

Much later I recalled how my mother's sobs transformed that beautiful movie star face of my memories into a ghost of despair. No one knew if we would ever see one another again, and although everyone hoped that the Americans would overthrow Fidel, it never happened. Meanwhile, my memory returns to me the terrifying face of my mother, crying out with a desperate scream, desperate but silent, the scream that I still carry inside me....

When it was time to go, Mami came very close to us as if she could give us a hug by touching her hands to the glass. But all her hands could do is touch the cold and flat surface of the aquarium and you could see the sweat in the palm of her hands. Then she began to cry and her face got all ugly and I got a knot in my throat, but the tears didn't come out because I thought that if I cried Mami would get even sadder. And I didn't want her to be sad....

My recollection of that little girl was one of a twelve-year-old who was off on an adventure to the USA, happy and enthusiastic. Later, it was my sister who told me that I did nothing but cry the entire time we traveled those famous ninety miles that separate Havana from the land of enchantment.

Salvador Longoria is a successful attorney, named "Outstanding Young Lawyer of 1991" by the Louisiana Bar Association. He came to the United States with his family as a young boy in 1962.

I was born in Bayamo—a city located in Oriente Province, Cuba—in 1958, and I came to the United States with my family when I was four years old.... I clearly remember the day we left Cuba. My parents, sisters, and I stood on our front lawn and said farewell to many friends. I knew something was wrong but did not comprehend any political implications. We got into a taxi that took us to the airport. I sat in the back-seat of the cab and watched the crowd walk to the other side of the street as they waved to us. It was an emotional moment for my family, but my thoughts were filled with the excitement of our forthcoming travels.

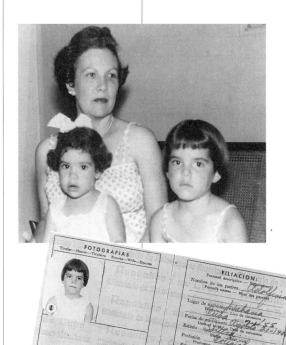

Margarita Gagliardi (at right) with her mother and sister in 1962, just before they left their home in Camagüey. Because their family was on a list of people forbidden to leave the island, Margarita's mother obtained false passports for them.

Margarita Sainz de la Peña Gagliardi came to the United States in 1962 with her mother and sister. The Castro government discouraged professionals from leaving the country by refusing to grant exit visas. Margarita, whose mother was a teacher, described how her family managed to leave Cuba.

My parents were divorced when I was four years old. So in this whole story my mother is the hero. In order to get us out of the country, since our family was one that they didn't particularly want to leave, she went to the Swiss embassy and got false passports for herself, my sister, and me. We left the country on a regular Pan Am flight, but under assumed names and with the false passports.

That was July 14, 1962. Which is also Bastille Day, so it's my liberation day as well. At this particular point in time, the Castro regime was being very selective about the people they were permitting to leave the country. We were people that in fact were on the list not to let out of the country, for political and economic reasons.

It's a strange thing for a seven-year-old to be told that you can't tell anybody what your name is—that you're not this person, you're now that person. That's what happened during the two weeks prior to leaving while the passports and other paper work were being arranged. I was a pretty spaced-out little kid when we arrived in Miami. I think I developed ulcers by the time I was seven.

Actually, I should tell you one other thing. My grandmother had made for my sister and me pairs of earrings. When we were leaving the country, my mother told the customs that they were from the five-and-dime. They were in our ears anyway, so that was the only piece of jewelry we left the country with. I still have those too. They were the only physical objects we had when we got here.

Roberto Ortiz, who came to the United States in 1962, described how local revolutionary committees made leaving Cuba a complicated process.

People started getting disappointed—leaving. My cousin was the first one out. Then my sister came four months before I came. I came in '62. It was getting rougher and rougher to leave. It took five years for my mother to get out. Things started getting rougher and rougher, and as time went on, the more places you got to check with, more people you got to clear with. They just wanted to bother you and make it rough for you.

People didn't know what was going to happen. When you left the county after '60, you could not leave anything to anybody. You are supposed to turn everything to the government. The moment you submit the papers, you're not supposed to get anything out of the house. On every block they had a watching committee, watching everything you do. These people will watch you twenty-four hours a day, all your move-

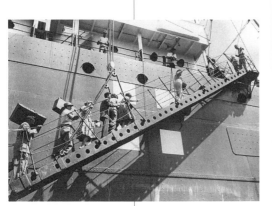

Refugees board a ship in Cuba in May 1963. It had carried supplies to Cuba, sent by the U.S. government in exchange for the release of prisoners captured in the Bay of Pigs invasion. On its return to the United States, the ship carried 751 Cubans to Port Everglades, Florida.

ments. When you leave, everything that you left inside—a watching committee would come and make an inventory and seal the house. They'd put paper in there with glue on the door and lock them up. And that was the end of it. You lose everything. Whatever was inside, it's the government property.

So a lot of people sneak things out of the house, and my house was like a clearinghouse. Everybody was bringing stuff in there to keep, so we had stuff from three or four or more different families. All the furniture and record players—smaller things, all kinds of stuff—could be taken out of the house at night, so the watching committee didn't see it. Was brought into my house, because we weren't leaving. We were just watching it for them, you see—in storage for them, that's all, in case Castro fails and they come back....

It took me ninety days waiting to get out. I'll never forget when I went to get vaccinated. They put me in line with thirteen or fourteen people. And they got a piece of cloth with alcohol on it, and the first guy on line got lucky, because he got the clean cotton. But the second guy got a little bit of the other guy, and when that cotton reached the last guy in line, you got everybody's dirt in your arm.

I was allowed to bring one suit, three pairs of everything—undershirts, underwear, socks—and one towel and toothpaste and a shaving kit, and that's it. Everything else is government property. They were searching in the airport.

Felisa Colon left Cuba when she was 22. Later, she described the problems she faced after deciding to leave.

My father was from Canton [China]. He went to Cuba when he was eighteen years old. He married and stayed there until the Revolution came. The Chinese Cubans all left Cuba for the United States right after the Revolution. It was commonly said that the Chinese Cubans all recognized Castro as a Communist from the start. On the day the Revolution began, my father said, "This is communism, I just know."...

It was very difficult to leave Cuba. We made the application to leave in 1964, and they sent me to a farm as punishment. I worked twenty-seven months in the fields doing all kinds of things, cutting sugar cane, planting trees, cleaning up the fields. They paid me twenty-one cents an hour; it rained, they didn't pay us. It was more like emotional punishment, real hard work. But it was a good experience. I met many, many people who now are living in different parts of the United States. I always know somebody somewhere—you ought to see my telephone bill.

Father Félix Varela

The first Cuban political refugee to live in the United States was Father Félix Varela. Born in Havana in 1788, Varela was orphaned at the age of six. He was sent to St. Augustine, Florida, to live with his grandfather, an officer in the Spanish garrison there.

When Varela was 14, he broke with his family's military tradition and decided to be a priest. "I wish to be a soldier of Jesus Christ," he wrote. "I do not wish to kill men. I wish rather to save their souls."

He returned to Cuba and entered the San Carlos Seminary. After his ordination in 1810, Varela taught classes in music. His writings on philosophy, politics, and science won him a reputation as a brilliant scholar. In 1821, he was appointed one of Cuba's representatives in the Spanish Cortes, or parliament.

In the Cortes, Father Varela called on the government to recognize the independence of the recently liberated Spanish-American republics. For Cuba, he asked for self-rule within the Spanish empire and an end to slavery. These ideas were far too progressive for the time, and Varela was forced to flee Spain in 1823.

For the rest of his life, Varela lived in the United States, where he founded a Spanish-language newspaper called *El Habanero* (a *habanero* is a man from Havana), which addressed cultural and social issues and advocated the cause of Cuban independence. Copies of it were smuggled into Cuba, and the governor of Cuba hired an assassin to kill Varela. But Varela confronted the assassin and persuaded him not to commit such an evil act.

Varela was assigned to a parish in New York City, where many Irish immigrants lived. He became a spokesman for their needs, standing up to anti-Catholic bigots. He opened schools for both girls and boys. During a cholera epidemic in 1832, Varela visited the immigrant ships infested with the disease to bring the sacraments to sufferers.

When his health deteriorated, Varela returned to Florida. He spent his last years in St. Augustine, now part of the United States. He died there in 1853. Years later, José Martí acknowledged Varela's contributions to the Cuban independence movement: "He was the man who taught us how to think."

ESCAPES

Many Cuban refugees fled to a third country before entering the United States. Maria Luisa Salcines and her family went to Spain.

When we reached Madrid (May 27, 1963), a Cuban refugee organization was waiting for us. They found us a place to stay and fed us two meals a day. Cuban doctors, lawyers, teachers, and businessmen, everybody worked at the center helping to serve food or distributing clothing. During this time my father did all sorts of odd jobs so that he could raise money for our trip to the United States. One of those jobs was working as an extra in the movie, *The Fall of the Roman Empire....*

My maternal grandfather was a Spaniard who had emigrated to Cuba during the Spanish Civil War [1936–39]. He was born in the outskirts of Barcelona.... A week after we arrived in Madrid my father put us on a train and sent us to Barcelona.

Mother couldn't stop crying, and we cried with her. I remember feeling scared on the train and sitting very close to her and my little brother. My mother had never met her cousin Pau and she carried a picture of him so that when we reached the train station we could find him.

A makeshift raft carries Cuban refugees through the Straits of Florida, about 45 miles from Key West, in August 1994. They had been at sea for more than two days, and one of them had collapsed from the heat.

Mother was terrified. What if her cousin didn't show up? Where would we go with no money? On the train we met an elderly man who asked my mother what was wrong. Between sobs she explained her situation and he being a typical Spaniard, assured her that if no one picked us up at the station we could stay with his family.

When we reached Barcelona it was the middle of the night. The station was packed with people. Mother kept looking at her picture but we couldn't find her cousin. Finally after people began to leave the station we saw Pau Boada. He was also holding a picture of my mother and when they saw each other, mother ran into his arms and they both began to cry.

A medical student named William was the sole survivor of a group of eight people who fled Cuba in a raft in November 1972. He gave the following account of his escape.

By day, when there was no sun, there were the waves that made us hang on to one another to avoid falling overboard. You can imagine how it was at night. The cold made us huddle against one another and cover ourselves with the driest clothing we had. Then the moment arrived. When the raft fell apart all of us took whatever tires and wood we could because we needed to hold on to something in order to survive....

Mrs. Cosme had carried [her] dog with her, burdened by the task of keeping it from falling overboard. You can imagine that when she had to hang on to a tire, there was no way left except, with grief in her heart, to let the dog swim alone. The poor thing swam with us the best it could, with its head above the water. When it could not do so anymore, we saw it moving away from us little by little until it disappeared....

The hour arrived when death began to surround us.... The first to die was Dr. Tasis—almost in front of me. I saw on his face that he was doing his utmost. Suddenly raising his voice, he said, "William, son, I can't do any more. I hope God—" And he disappeared in that instant before our eyes through the center of the tire that he was using as a life preserver....

Then night enveloped us. The breeze blew gently and we slept a little.... Our remaining little group tried as much as possible to stay together in a circle, using the rest of the raft and tires to support ourselves.

When morning came, a dense fog began to enclose us. The sun appeared faintly on the horizon. Suddenly I felt someone pulling me strongly by my clothes, saying to me, "William, I believe my time has come. I am sinking fast.... Save my mother for me...."

Little by little Dr. Huerte began to move farther away into the middle of that gentle mist. One can imagine that he withdrew from us to prevent our having to witness his death. His mother burst into tears and began making superhuman efforts to save him. She tried futilely to hold him up. But he was completely exhausted and there was little or nothing I could do....

A U.S. soldier stands guard at the military base at Guantánamo Bay. Sometimes Cubans sought to cross the barbed wire to obtain asylum. In 1994, the U.S. government temporarily kept thousands of refugees at the base before allowing them to enter the United States.

This inner tube is the remains of the raft that eight people and a dog used to leave Cuba in 1972. One of the refugees tells his story in the account on this page.

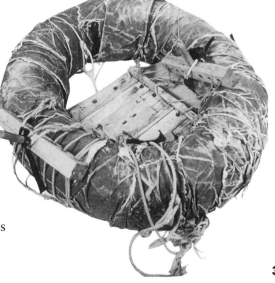

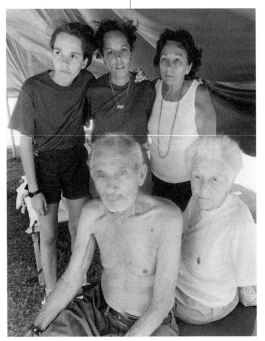

During the Mariel boatlift, Lazaro H. Fernández in Key West rented a shrimp boat and went to Mariel, where he picked up his brother, sister-in-law, and their children. Port officials issued this certificate, which permitted the boat to leave. The "cargo" is listed as lastre, *which means "a heavy object that can be used as ballast and thrown overboard when necessary."*

Four generations of a family of Cuban refugees at the U.S. base at Guantánamo Bay in 1994 wait to be transported to the United States. In the foreground are 84-year-old Julio de la Torre and his wife, Evangelina. In back, from the left, are their great-granddaughter Yaimairi Diaz Rodriguez, granddaughter Nancy Rodriguez de la Torre, and daughter Dulce de la Torre.

The situation became even more desperate. Now I had the responsibility of caring for the doctor's mother and my own safety.... Hanging on to the tires and boards that surrounded us...I made another small, moveable raft with the tires and planks. Laboriously I got on it and with great effort pulled her up against me.... The thing now was to survive.

The sun, burning ferociously, made us delirious. At times I woke up and it was dark. At other times I woke up and there was light.... We were hidden by waves; besides, we had nothing, nothing with color that could stand out and distinguish us at a distance. We had to trust ourselves to luck, and pray.... Thus the first day passed. On the second I heard a muffled sound. I could not imagine that Mrs. Cosme's end was nearing. At times I was trying to hold her and move her, but her strength was failing. I cannot forget the look on her face and her gratitude. Her eyes spoke more than words. She had struggled hard to keep herself and the others alive, and now she, too, was dying.

Suspecting the end but still making an effort, she said to me, "Fight for your life and try to save yourself, son. If you succeed, tell all of this journey so that the world is informed. We died trying to be free. God wants you to succeed, son. Thank you. I am going to sleep a little. Don't wake me." And thus she entered her eternal sleep....

I believe it was God's will that I survived.... I knew someone had to endure to bear witness. This idea stayed with me during the remaining days I had to survive until a fisherman found me.

A man named Rolando escaped to the American naval base at Guantánamo Bay in 1972. To prevent such escapes, the Cuban government had surrounded the base with three fortified fences. Rolando told his story to an interviewer in 1977.

We waited all afternoon at the first fence, hiding and watching the movements around us. I can still remember the cold. With our binoculars we observed the passing of the guards. There was no moon that night and by eleven we began to cross the first fence. It had about five inches between the horizontal wires.... Looking upward, we noted that the higher you went, the more space there was between these wires, but never more than six inches....

We had brought heavy ropes with us. Crouching on the ground, we used them to pry apart the wires at the bottom of the fence so we could crawl through. In this way we safely passed the first fence and crossed the road. But if we had walked straight ahead, we would have been seen by the guards. Stretched out flat, we rolled along the ground until we reached the second fence. Here we proceeded in the same way, and again at the next fence. Then we came to the minefield.

Along the ground we came across a very thin wire so fine you could hardly see it. We noticed it because of the reflections from it were visible from our close-up position. The wire is at-

A Coast Guard seaman offers his hand to Cuban refugees picked up in the Straits of Florida. Because the trip was so hazardous, many people died at sea if they were not spotted by a Coast Guard vessel.

tached to a detonator and when you break the wire at any point, it explodes. Carefully feeling our way along, we came to the next series of fences, where there is less surveillance. Remember that we had been eating next to nothing for a long time and that for the past two days we had had no food or water. Our lips were so parched that they were cracking....

As soon as we passed the remaining fences we saw the American guards. On their side they patrol in jeeps, since there's a greater distance between the sentry posts than on the Cuban side. A few more meters and we reached the American fence, a Peerless chain-link. We climbed over the top and in our joy cried out, "Finally, we've reached freedom!"

Hamlet Arias was eight years old when his grandmother brought him to the United States on the Mariel boatlift. He recalled the journey.

It was night. All that I remember, because I was so small, was my grandmother grabbing me by the arm, grabbing some of my clothes, putting them in a bag with some papers, and running out the door. We tried to take my older sister, but she had two kids and couldn't come....

We were the last people to get on this boat.... It was just a fishing boat, built to hold about 50 people, but not for traveling across the ocean. There were many more people on this boat on that trip. Holding onto the sails, on top of the roof of the cabin, holding onto the sides of the boat.

There were other people on *lanchitas*, which are little boats that are not meant to go too far offshore.... But the soldiers on other boats shot them down. I remember hearing a lot of gunfire, a lot of chasing, boats sinking. I saw about six or seven boats sink. I saw a person eaten by a shark....

In the daytime my grandmother stood over me the whole time so that I wouldn't get sunburned. I was seasick. All we had to eat were crackers and water. At night, it was pitch black. All you could see was the moon and its reflection.... I remember that somebody threw a wrapper from a cracker into the sea, and somebody jumped overboard and got it.... By the second night, we arrived at Miami.

These are some of the 125,000 people who survived the dangerous voyage across the Straits of Florida to freedom in 1980. As they arrive in a crowded boat at Key West, the strain shows on their faces.

Cubans disembark from a plane in Miami in 1966. This was the time of the "freedom flights," when more than 300,000 Cubans left their homeland via air from Varadero, Cuba.

CHAPTER THREE

PORTS OF ENTRY

n the 1820s, when the first Cuban immigrants arrived in the United States, the federal government allowed each state to make its own immigration laws and policies. In the 19th century, most Cubans disembarking in New York, Boston, Philadelphia, and New Orleans were allowed entry because the majority were merchants, well-educated political refugees, or skilled workers.

Far to the south, in Key West, there were no regulations barring immigrants until the late 19th century. Indeed, for many years Key West had closer ties to Cuba than to the United States, for the only way to reach it was by sea. Long before a railroad linked Key West with northern cities, there was a regular ferry-boat service between it and Havana. Cubans who wanted to work in Key West simply bought a ticket.

With the establishment of Cuban cigar factories in Florida and New York City in the 1860s and 1870s, immigration started to increase. Still, by 1900 there were only about 11,000 U.S. citizens of Cuban descent. Fifty years later, the figure was 33,000, nearly half of whom lived in New York City. Florida was a distant second with about 8,000 Cuban American citizens.

When the huge influx of Cuban refugees began in 1959, the vast majority went to Florida. The city of Miami had mushroomed in size during the 1920s as a tourist attraction. Among those who went there for vacations were wealthy Cubans, who often flew over for weekend shopping sprees. Thus, when upper-class Cubans became the first refugees from Castro's Cuba, they chose Miami as their destination. Believing that Castro would soon be overthrown, they wanted to stay in a familiar place where the weather was much like Cuba's.

The U.S. government eagerly embraced the refugees and established a Cuban Refugee Center in Miami to process them. In 1966, the U.S. Congress passed the Cuban American Adjustment Act, which gave any Cuban who had resided in the United States for a year the right to become a permanent resident. Hundreds of thousands of Cubans who have arrived since 1966 have taken advantage of this provision, which has not been granted to any other immigrant group.

In addition, the U.S. government has supplied financial aid to help Cuban refugees find homes and start businesses. During the Kennedy administration, a Cuban Refugee Program began to resettle some of the newcomers to areas of the country outside Florida.

The difficulty in leaving Cuba has varied according to the changes in Castro's emigration policy. It was relatively easy for the "golden exiles" from 1959 to 1962 to leave. Castro thought their departure would get rid of those most likely to stage a rebellion against his government. He dubbed the emigrants *gusanos*, or "worms."

Later, Castro tightened the process for Cubans to obtain visas and plane tickets. Generally, young men 15 and older were refused permission to leave because they were eligible for the military draft. Since 1988, however, the number of Cubans granted permission to leave has risen from about 3,600 a year to more than 66,000.

Not all were able to leave, however, because at the same time the United States has tried to cut back on Cuban immigration. The enormous numbers of Cubans arriving in Florida put a strain on the country's ability to absorb them.

The administrations of Presidents George Bush and Bill Clinton reduced the number of Cubans the United States would accept. In 1995, Clinton announced that the United States would no longer admit *balseros* (rafters) seeking refuge— although Cubans applying for visas in Havana would be considered. It remains to be seen whether Clinton or any future U.S. President will in fact turn back large numbers of Cubans fleeing their native land.

EARLY SETTLEMENTS

Cuban fishermen in Key West in 1886 show a prize catch—a green turtle. The word key comes from the Spanish cayo, which means "small island." Key West is closer to Cuba than to the Florida mainland, and from the time of its founding in the early 1800s, many Cubans have settled there.

Around 1904, a Florida sponge fisherman told his life story to an interviewer for an American magazine. The fisherman was the son of a Cuban mother and a British sailor. When he was five, his father died in a shipwreck, and his mother took the family to Key West, where her brother lived.

I've come to know that Key West is a strange town unlike any other. There's an English part to it, and a Spanish part, the Spanish being bigger, but poorer, and alas! much dirtier. Several languages are spoken in the town; Spanish most of all, it seems to me. But, above everything else, our island-town is American; that's why so much money is made and lost in it, and so many business enterprises spring up....

One day, when my uncle came home from a long cruise I ran down to the wharf to meet him. But for an hour he was too busy to notice me. He was talking excitedly to José and Manuel Silvas, two turtlers [turtle fishermen] we knew well and they were handling and passing back and forth...some wet, dirty-looking objects that I did not recognize. When I got very close I found out that these dirty objects smelt very bad. How well I've come to know that smell in the half of a hundred years that's rolled over my head since then. Most of the months of those years I've been out on the water, with the deck of my boat piled up with these same dark-looking, nasty-smelling objects.

For, you see, these were sponges that José and his brother had found out on the reefs when they were looking for turtles; and they were showing them to my uncle because his judgment and knowledge were much respected among all the sea-faring people that came in to the Key West wharves. The Silvas brothers kept telling my uncle over and over that there were wide fields of this strange growth out in the waters they had been turtling in, and my uncle, Alejandro Piestra, was running forward in his mind to the possibility of harvesting these and finding a paying market for them. Small as the incident appeared, a great United States industry had its beginnings right there.

As nearly as I can remember this happened about 1853 or 1854, and within a few months my uncle had fitted out two or three small boats for the sponging fields of José and Manuel. I was scarcely eleven years old, but he put me on one of the boats.

"It's going to be a money-making business, Elena," said he to my mother, in his far-seeing way; "not now, perhaps, but one of these days. Let the boy learn it from the start and grow into it."

Until 1960, the largest Cuban American community was in New York City. Many Cuban immigrants lived and worked with the Puerto Ricans of the city. In the 19th century, New York's Cuban community strongly supported the cause of Cuban independence. Bernardo Vega, a Puerto Rican, recalled the arrival of Cuba's great revolutionary leader, José Martí, two years after the end of the Ten Years' War.

It was on January 3, 1880, in the middle of that bitter winter, that José Martí arrived in New York. Shortly after, it was announced that he would be speaking at Steck Hall. And in his first public appearance he captured the hearts of the Antillean exiles [those from the Antilles, the island chain that includes both Puerto Rico and Cuba]. His eloquence and logic were convincing. It was correct to continue struggling for the cause of independence.... A new wave of hope began to swell in the breasts of the emigrant community.

Martí was made president of the Comité Revolucionario Cubano on May 13, 1880.... But the committee did not make much headway. Its newspaper, *La Revolución*...ceased publication. In the whole United States the only [Cuban] paper that continued to come out was *Yara*, which was published in Key West.... Its support came from the *tabaqueros* [cigar makers] in Key West and Tampa....

[In 1888] the Liga de Artesanos [the league of artisans] was founded. Its aims were mostly cultural and civic.... The Liga Antillana, a similar organization but made up of women, was also formed at that time. Its Cuban and Puerto Rican members belonged to the working class.... It was the first such society with Cuban and Puerto Rican members ever founded in New York. It was organized by women who were related to cigarworkers....

It is worth mentioning that the group was completely interracial, with all its activities shared by white, black, and mulatto women. Because they were a mixed group, most of the

This Cuban-owned bar in the Tampa area around 1890 was a place where both men and women could socialize, and coffee was as likely as alcohol to be the beverage of choice.

Emigrés never forgot their homeland. This couple from Ybor City had their picture taken in Cuban patriotic costumes.

meeting halls shut their doors to them, which is why they usually held their events in places provided by the Socialist Party or the Cigarworkers' Union.

In the 19th and early 20th centuries, many Cuban workers and artisans traveled back and forth from Cuba and the United States. Dr. M. Santos, who was interviewed in the 1930s, recalled this period.

I came to Tampa [in 1894] and saw an electric street car. The impression that it gave me was that how could a street car move without horses. I would stand up on the seat and would ask my mother where were the horses, and she would tell me that they were behind the street car. The first thing I did when I stepped down was to go running to see where the horses were....

I remember...when war was declared between the United States and Spain. We used to holler through the streets, "Hurrah for McKinley" [then President of the United States]. I also remember that they used to sell certain post cards with the *Maine* [U.S. battleship that was blown up in Havana harbor] painted [on them]. One would place the fire from a cigarette on one [end of the card]. The fire would travel until it reached the *Maine*, and produce an explosion....

When I lacked two months to have 18 years, I went to New York with two friends. These friends did not know English and I was the interpreter.... I stayed there some three months. I visited the museums of the city, the Museum of Natural History, the Aquarium, where I was much impressed by the "Hippocampo" or marine horse [seahorse]. I also saw Caruso sing at the Grand Opera. Also the Flat Iron Building. Another thing that impressed me very much was the hour of the rush at the City Hall, down town, in order to take the subway. I also saw the Brooklyn Bridge.

Ybor City, Florida, the "Cigar City," developed a multiethnic culture and way of life with the arrival of cigar makers from Cuba, Spain, and Italy. A man identified only as "a mulatto" told an interviewer collecting oral histories in the 1930s for the Works Progress Administration about this culture.

As to the customs here: This was once a small Cuba.... In the feasts of Christmas-day, there were many "rhumbitas" [rumbas, Cuban dances] on the streets. I remember that we formed rhumbas in the house of Puebla. We were one week "rhumbaring" [an Ybor City term meaning "to have a good time"]. We would come out of the factory, and go to the house of Puebla to continue the rhumba, and thus day after day....

Christmas Eve was celebrated with much merriment. The Three Wise Men bring the toys in Cuba on January 6th, but it was never celebrated here in this way. They always come on Christmas Eve.

They were also accustomed to burning the old year here. The people would get together in many groups, and they would symbolize the old year with a puppet so that the coming new year would be better. As the puppet was being burned, they would say: "Go, evil year, so that the coming one is better."...

I remember that I and several more would go to Port Tampa to fish, and every day we would catch a shark. At 5:15 on the dot they would come in troops. It really seemed that they had a clock, as they did not vary a single minute. One would entrap himself every time. I would wrap the rope around my arm, and would pull, holding on to a pole, until I would draw his head from the water. Then my companion would sledge-hammer his head with an iron bar that "not even the Chinese doctor" [an Ybor City expression that arose in Cuba because of the skill of Chinese doctors on the island] could revive him. But one day when I caught a shark which was as big as this porch, he pulled so hard that he "almost carried my arm." The rope remained marked on my arm for one week.... Since then I do not catch any more sharks....

I also remember a very large lagoon.... They had taken that as a dump pile, and all the shore was filled up with cans. It seems that an alligator had the custom of coming there to eat the refuse.

One day I went to this large lagoon, but it seems that the alligator saw me first. I had my back turned to him when I heard a terrible noise among the cans.

I looked backward and I see that piece of alligator who was after me. I...ran as I have never run before in my life. I did not stop running until I had reached home.... I do not know if it is true, but they say that these animals run very much.

Students at the San Carlos Institute, a school in Key West, pay tribute to José Martí, the Cuban liberator, in a pageant held around 1908. Martí's image appears in the background.

LATER ARRIVALS

A man kisses the ground—in this case, the concrete on the pier—as he arrives in Florida around 1966. By that time, many Cubans had come to regard Castro's regime as intolerable.

A Red Cross worker distributes cups of milk to Cuban refugees arriving at Port Everglades, Florida, in April 1963. U.S. government agencies also helped to resettle the new arrivals from Cuba.

Pablo Medina came to New York City in 1960 with his family. Coming from the warmth of Cuba, they were startled to find that it was snowing in New York. In his Exiled Memories, *Medina wrote about the experience.*

Snow. Everywhere the snow and air so cold it cracks and my words hang stiffly in the air like cartoons. After that first stunning welcome of the New York winter, I rush down the steps of the plane and sink my bare hands into the snow, press it into a ball, and throw it at my sister. I miss by a few yards. The snowball puffs on the ground. I make another and miss again. Then I can make no more, for my hands are numb. I look down at them: red and wet, they seem disembodied, no longer mine. A few flakes land on them, but these flakes are not the ones I know from *Little Lulu* or *Archie* [comic books of the 1950s]; they are big limpy things that melt soon after landing. On closer look, I can make out the intricate crystals, small and furry and short lived. As if from a great distance, I hear my mother calling. Her voice seems changed by the cold and the words come quicker, in shorter bursts, as if there might be a limited supply of them. I follow the family into the airport building. It is early February. It is El Norte.

The drive into Manhattan is a blur. We piled into a cab and took a wide and busy highway in, most probably the Grand Central Parkway. Once over the East River, my first impression was of riding down into a canyon, much of it shadowy and forbidding, where the sky, steel gray at the time, was a straight path like the street we were on, except bumpier and softer: old cotton swabbed in mercury. It seemed odd that out of that ominous ceiling came the pure white snow I had just touched.

Cristina Garcia, author of the novel Dreaming in Cuban, *came to New York City in 1961. She described her parents' feelings when they arrived in the United States.*

When my parents left Cuba in 1961, they thought it was only a temporary move. They gave Fidel Castro six months at most and expected to return to their homeland once the whole revolution business blew over. We lived for a while in a nice hotel overlooking Central Park—and waited.

The money began running out faster than my parents anticipated, so we moved to shabbier and shabbier hotels, until we all slept in one tiny room someplace that apparently rented on a

very short-term basis. My mother saw flamboyantly dressed
women hastily escorting men down the corridor night after
night, until she finally decided it was time to move on.

*Margarita Sainz de la Peña Gagliardi arrived in Miami in 1962,
when she was seven. The Red Cross and the Refugee Relocation
Service were two of the agencies that helped the newcomers.*

The thing I remember the most was the box that I got
from the Red Cross. The Red Cross used to put together these little boxes that had a toothbrush, toothpaste, a little toy and so forth. There was a box of crayons
inside, something to entertain us. I still have the box. It was
really the only thing that we had because we literally left with
two changes of clothes and that was it.

They took care of all our medical needs and dental needs.
Because a lot of people didn't speak the language, they didn't
have referrals to physicians, and this was a public service that
was provided at the refugee centers.

The Refugee Relocation Service in Miami found us temporary housing in Miami. I think we were in somewhat of a
unique situation in that my mother already spoke English and
had academic training. She was a teacher, and they helped to lo-
cate her in a school in Miami. She initially started out in the library there. Later she continued her teaching profession. We
settled in southwest Miami and had a nice little house.

In 1965, Castro permitted people with relatives in the United States to leave from the port of Camarioca. Cuban exiles brought them across in small boats. These women and children disembark in Key West.

In August 1994, a sudden rush of balseros, *or "rafters," began to cross the Straits of Florida. President Bill Clinton ordered them to be held first in a detention center near Miami (where this picture was taken), and later at Guantánamo. The man at left holds the compass he used to navigate across the sea. His friend has drawn on the back of his shirt the word* balsero, *a compass, and a raft.*

Sofia Rodriguez was a principal in a school in Cuba. After Castro started nationalizing the schools, she and her husband and three daughters came to Miami. The U.S. government sponsored resettlement programs to help Cuban refugees find jobs in other parts of the country.

When we arrived in Miami, my husband and I went to the refugee center. We completed the applications and looked for work. He was a lawyer and I was a teacher. They called us after some time, and they said there was an opportunity in Bluffton, Indiana. There was a church that wanted to sponsor a Cuban family and a high school that needed a Spanish teacher. There was our opportunity, even though we didn't know where Bluffton, Indiana, was. We had heard of the Indianapolis 500 and located Bluffton two fingers above the Indianapolis [on the] map.

In 1962 Rodolfo de León, age 11, went to Miami with his brother and mother. His father followed a year later. Rodolfo remembered the shock of his arrival.

The people who were waiting for us—they were opportunistic, *stupid, low-down rats*! They were the worst kind of people you can imagine. My father had sent money over here for us. The dollar was going very high on the black market. So my father had to pay I don't know how many Cuban *pesos* for a dollar. [He had sent] about $400 in different installments many times. We only got $200. These people were *stealing* it. They didn't give us any money. This was the only reference we had here. They were friends of [a friend]. They had done that before. They had "taken care of" people, sons who came.

We stayed at their house, two weeks, three weeks. My mother couldn't stand it. We went to bed hungry.

The second or third week we were here we started receiving help from the government. We collected some food, and we got $100 a month. We rented one place first. The rent was...way too high. The rent was $95. We had five dollars left for the month.

After a month or something like that we found this other place, which was $72. We were renting the apartment for $72, and so we had $28 for the month. That meant a dollar a day. We lived on that for I think about a year and a half. Aside from my mother baby-sitting for about two dollars for six hours, that was the only income we had.

I remember in that place we had only one pillow. One day my brother and I started fighting for the pillow. We really got into a brawl about it. I started chasing him. My mother was chasing us. Then my mother broke down crying. We stopped. I really felt bad.

A man who gave his name as Agustín described his escape to the United States in the late 1970s. After a dangerous trip in a boat, he and his companions were picked up by an American ship with a Cuban crew. He described his arrival in Florida.

By the time we arrived, we were out of gas. One of the men came from the other boat and asked if the adults had eaten. I said no, that we had given all the food to the children. Another guy called out, "We have plenty of fish here," and they started throwing fish, and fish, and fish into our boat! After we cleaned it, we fried the fish and ate our first meal.

A helicopter flew over us and the other boat signaled it. In a little while a green light began flashing at us. I asked what it was, because I was afraid. They explained it was a ship from the Coast Guard and I relaxed. The people on the other boat told the Coast Guard about us and they towed both boats. By then it was eleven o'clock at night and we were about six miles from Key West. We had been on the sea for twenty-four hours. When we arrived at Key West we received wonderful attention. I never imagined we would have such a welcome. We were surprised at our reception here because the Cuban government had deceived us. They told us Cubans in the States were living in terrible conditions and starving to death. I was so overwhelmed by the way we were treated here that I walked away from everybody for a while and wept.

In 1980, eight-year-old Hamlet Arias arrived in Miami on the Mariel boatlift. He remembered that learning English was no problem for him.

My recollection of how many days we stayed in Miami is hazy because I was so young. We lined up, and people gave us little bags. My bag had shaving cream and a razor. And little books, like a Bible.

For some reason, I remember that I understood every word anybody said to me, even though it was in English. Clear as day. In Cuba I used to pretend I spoke English. I would invent words, and say, "I know that's an English word." That was one of the games my friend and I played.

In Miami, they took us to this base, where we slept in big hangars, with beds lined up. Some people slept outside in tents. We stayed there maybe one or two nights, I can't remember how long. I remember playing with some girl who was there, just running around. Then my mother, who was in Florida, met us. She had arranged that we would go on a bus to New York, and right away my mother, my grandmother, and I got on the bus.

The transition between Spanish and English was so fast for me. I didn't even realize that I had switched languages altogether. It just came natural to me. My mother told me that when I started school I was in a bilingual class, but the next day they put me in an all-English class. That was later, in New York.

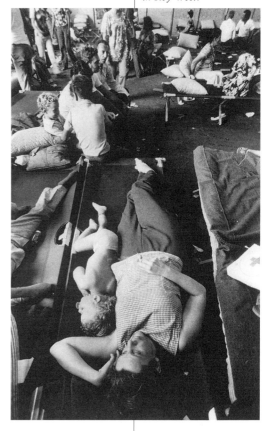

The Mariel boatlift of 1980 brought about 125,000 refugees from Cuba in less than six months. Many had to be temporarily housed in shelters, such as this one in Key West.

In 1963, an unidentified Cuban leaves the U.S. government's refugee center in Miami. Nicknamed Freedom Tower, the center offered the refugees help in finding jobs and housing.

FIRST EXPERIENCES

Adjusting to a culture in which the language was English was one of the first problems of the Spanish-speaking Cubans. Seventeen-year-old Desi Arnaz, who came to Miami with his father in 1934, recalled his experience with it.

I walked around and found what looked like a modest restaurant but nice and clean. A real cute waitress brought me a menu. I looked up, said, "Thank you," and opened it. After looking it over, I began cursing the Jesuits [who had taught me in high school]. Not only had they failed to teach me how to understand or speak English, they had not even taught me how to read it. The waitress was standing by my side with pad and pencil. I looked at her and smiled again. She looked at me, smiled back and said something that sounded like, "Areyouabouttoorderyourdinnernow?"

That's the trouble with a foreign language, you see; nobody stops in between words.... Anyway, not wanting to let her stand there any longer, I pointed to four different lines of the menu, and wound up with four different kinds of soups, which I ate or drank...as if this were what I normally ordered for dinner. I thought she had looked kind of funny when I first pointed to the four different lines on the menu, and by the time she brought me the second plate of soup, I knew why. You must remember that in 1934 there were very few Cubans in Miami.... A week later I found one small restaurant with a sign which said, "*Se habla Español*" ["Spanish spoken"]. Today, with the half-million or more exiles in that same area of Miami, you are lucky if you can find one that says "English spoken."

Marisella Veiga came to the United States as a very young girl. She described her initial fear of English.

One autumn afternoon in 1962 I learned how to speak English. Certainly, I had heard the language spoken before. My father used it with the Lauer family who had given our family a home for a month that August when we moved to Minnesota from Miami. We lived in their farm house's basement. My brother Luis, two years older, had started second grade; he had attended first grade in Miami. He knew English. So did the teacher and students at the public school in St. Paul, where I reluctantly attended kindergarten.

On the day I learned English, I was looking up and out through our garden apartment window. We lived in a nice yellow brick building, one of dozens that formed the Sibly Manor Apartments.

I told my mother I wanted to go outside to play. She saw I stayed inside.

"Why don't you? Luis is playing with all the children," she said.

"He speaks English. I don't know how," I said.

"Go anyway," she said.

I obeyed. During that play session in the courtyard shared by several buildings, I ran with my brother and some neighborhood children. At one point, I stopped. The language made sense to me!

From that day on, I spoke English.

Not all early experiences in the United States were happy ones. Loyda Renta and her husband and son arrived in New York in 1980. She entered a program in Michigan for English-language training. In the first year, tragedy struck.

Everything was going along fine. But in life there are days of sun, but there are also days of intense fog and these came to us faster than we could have imagined. It was a fatal automobile accident, when our only son, who had just had his twelfth birthday, ceased to exist. Yes, exactly three months after we arrived, on December 26, 1980, we had an accident at 9:30 P.M., a tragic accident, and in that, well, my son died. It had been a month since he had had his twelfth birthday...and...that for me was *un choque* [a terrible blow], because beginning with that moment, I kind of had an aversion to the language, to the place, everything that related to my son—to the snow. It was snowing. The accident was caused primarily by the terrible fog and also by the careless way in which the truck driver was driving. With the great amount of fog, he should not have been driving at that speed. The majority of the passengers were injured, but the only one that died was my son.

For Cuban refugees who settled in northern areas of the United States, the first snowfall was memorable. Margarita Gagliardi (at left) with her mother and sister moved to Elkhart, Indiana, in 1964. "We loved the snow," Margarita recalled. "I think our neighbors thought we were wacky because we played so much in it."

Flora González Mandri arrived in the United States as part of the Pedro Pan program, in which children were sent out of Cuba by their parents. She lived with her aunt and went to Albertinum School in Ukiah, California. There are other Cuban children in her eighth-grade graduation picture in 1962. Flora is at the far right of the front row.

Sincerely, that for me was a terrible trauma. If we struggled to leave Cuba, mainly it was for our son. He was the one that was growing, the one who needed to form himself, and who had his entire life ahead of him. And then that...my mind...it was *un choque*...a very great shock.... I know that I traumatized myself a lot.

At that very moment, the direction of all our plans vanished. My husband as well as myself both lost control. We completed the school term very poorly, and we left that magnificent place. We left with the many memories that it brought us of our son.... Thanks to the good friends that God placed in our way, we were able to keep overcoming that tremendous crisis and find relief for that terrible pain that can be compared with none other in this world....

Yes, for me it was the end; it was an end from which I had to restore myself. Thanks to the many kind people who helped us—the very loving, expressive people—little by little, little bit by little bit, thanks be to God, we began to be restored. I recovered, but that trauma with the language did not go away. I still feel that I have it.

Writer and critic Gustavo Pérez Firmat remembered his first Christmas in Miami.

When we got to Miami in October 1960, we stopped celebrating Nochebuena [Christmas Eve]. It seemed pointless to observe this feast in exile, with our unsettled situation and the family scattered all over—some relatives still in Cuba and others in New York and Puerto Rico. The first Christmas in Miami we put up a tree, though a smaller and greener one, but the only crèche we could afford was a cardboard stable with fold-out figures. Instead of Nochebuena dinner, we had Christmas lunch; instead of the traditional roasted pig, Nena [my mother] baked a turkey. My parents kept hoping that we would be back in Cuba in time to celebrate Nochebuena the way we always had, but it didn't happen. Sitting around the table on Christmas Day, we weren't so much gloomy as dazed. We had been living in this house only a few weeks, everything was topsy-turvy, it wasn't clear what we were supposed to think or say. There we were, just my parents and us four children around the table, suddenly transformed into an American nuclear family. Instead of the noisy bacchanals we had been used to, our Christmas celebration was brief and muted. Earlier that morning Santa had left gifts for those of us who still believed in him, but two weeks later the Three Wise Men didn't show up.

Dr. Rosa Vazquez came to the United States with her parents and younger brother in 1961, when she was seven years old. She recalled her first experiences and the sense of being an exile.

My mother had two brothers living in New York, in the Bronx. They were working in factories and learning English. Julio was married and had two little girls, and we came to live at his house.

Soon after, every single uncle that had left Cuba came to live in this apartment in the Bronx. We were thirteen people living in this apartment with roaches. I went to a public school that had bars in the windows. And English—I didn't know a word of English. I had finished second grade in Cuba and was a really good student. I loved school. My mom was a teacher. And here I was in this school that was huge, where nobody understood me, and I didn't understand half of what was going on. I had been a student in a private school in Cuba in a special class where I was learning French, embroidery, piano— you know, rich-girl kind of school. And to go to that public school in the Bronx was a shock.

We came to live on Longfellow Avenue. If you go there now, it's devastated. But it wasn't that great in the '60s either. The first time I heard that they strangled somebody was on Longfellow Avenue. The first time that I knew what roach bombs were was on Longfellow Avenue. So my first encounter with New York City was devastating for me. It was devastating for my dad and my mom, who were both professionals. My mom went to a factory; she became a seamstress. And my dad started working in a factory in New Jersey making chairs. Essex County. Bloomfield area.

But all of us who lived in that apartment were tight. There was a lot of solidarity. But you know it was an embarrassment that was very weird for a little kid. The radio was on, the short-wave radio, trying to catch Cuba. The people on the radio said, "Castro is going to be out of Cuba in three days. Castro is going to be out of Cuba in four days. Castro is going to leave Cuba. So don't unpack your suitcases. Don't grow roots here, because you're leaving."

Maria Luisa Salcines, the child at right, came to the United States in 1964 with her parents and brother. They stayed with relatives in McAllen, Texas, until they could afford a home of their own.

Juliana Flores, who would settle permanently with her husband in the United States in 1956, came to Montreat College in North Carolina in 1949. She remembered her first impressions.

I was shy, had never been away from home before, and experienced the culture shock of making a transition from one culture to another. I was amazed at the little geographical knowledge many Americans have. They did not know where the island of Cuba was located. They thought it was an uncivilized place.

I was surprised at the freedom that young people had for dating. It was different than back home. Back home, my parents were there to solve my problems. It was expected that the children depend on the parents. When I came here, I learned that I had to think for myself. In Cuba, the parents do most of the thinking for the children and choose even the career. Sometimes they even bought the clothing for the young girls. So when I came here, I had to start thinking for myself and develop my independence. Here, you are a person and you cannot go out and ask somebody to make a decision for you. You have to think, and regardless of the decision, you have to go ahead. This is the most important thing in this culture: you have to think for yourself.

Ramon Fernandez came to the United States as a young boy in 1961. He remembered his impressions of the racial segregation that was practiced in Florida at the time.

In Cuba, you know, a person is black and you have mulattoes and things like that, but you go to the same restaurant that they go to and to pray in the same church they pray in; you never even think about it. We came here in 1961 and there were separate drinking fountains and everything. The blacks had to go to the back of the bus and things like that. I had a couple of black friends and I think they were very nice....

I remember one day getting into a bus, a crowded bus, and I'm sitting there, about ten to twelve years old, and this black lady comes on the bus and of course I wasn't even aware she was taught to sit in the back. So she comes into the door and I see a couple of people standing. I don't see any empty seats, so I get up to offer her my seat, and she just—she doesn't look at me, she looked right through me and she went right back to the back of the bus. I couldn't figure out what happened, why she didn't want to take my seat. Then I started getting wise when I looked in the back of the bus and all the blacks are sitting in the back.

Felisa Colon, of Chinese descent, left Cuba in the 1960s and settled in New York City. She described her first experiences.

I remember my family was very upset because I wouldn't eat when I first came. "Everybody comes here to eat, so how come you're not eating? That's why we're here." I didn't come here to eat; I came here for freedom, because I

Young men play basketball at Camp Libertad, a refugee detention center near Fort Walton Beach, Florida, in 1980. Part of the Mariel boatlift, they had little else to do but wait until the U.S. government completed their background checks to determine if they could stay in the United States.

like it. I couldn't eat because I was thinking about my friends who were in Cuba who didn't have food, and it was very, very sad to eat when you know that the people you care for didn't have anything to eat. I remember one time I passed out in the supermarket when I saw so many foods in one place. I tell the story now and people don't believe me—"How could you pass out in a supermarket?" And it was a very small neighborhood market. Had I gone to a larger one, I probably would be dead by now!

It was a cultural shock to come to the United States. It's like a little bird that gets freedom—you don't know where to go, what to do. I couldn't have enough, looking at the colors, bright, different. In Cuba we have very dull colors. Everybody wears about the same clothes, materials; you don't have the variety that we have here. And the garbage! I love the garbage in the United States; people put so many good things in there. In Cuba it is very clean because we don't throw out anything. You don't have disposable anything. You go to the market and buy eggs, you don't get them in an egg carton. You get eggs. I had a friend from Cuba last year—he came to New York to visit me—and I asked him, "What do you like most about America?" "The garbage! I expected to see the Statue of Liberty, but nobody told me about the garbage."

Sofia Rodriguez and her family found out when they arrived in Miami that a church in Bluffton, Indiana, wanted to sponsor a Cuban family. Sofia and her daughter Alicia remembered their first impressions of Bluffton.

Sofia: I didn't know what people in Indiana were going to expect. We were the first Cubans in the area, since Cubans didn't usually immigrate to small towns before Castro's time. My English was limited, but I had memorized two lines. I said them over and over: "Give me a chance, please, and I'll prove I can do it. Give me a chance."

Alicia: Well, we didn't know where we were going, but we knew we were going to go all together. So it was very nice and it was an adventure into the land of the cold and the snow, the boots and the gloves and the mittens. It was all a new adventure.

We found that the children in town were really curious about our family, the Cuban family that had arrived in town. I don't think that they knew what to expect. But they were always very helpful. They took us under their wings, and I was invited to all the kids' houses in town—to see what I looked like, I imagine. They helped me to learn English. They would come to our house the first week we were there and see what we were eating, if we wore shoes, if we knew how to use the phone, and if there was anything we needed. So I have fond memories of Bluffton and starting school there.

Most exiles fled Cuba without money or possessions and frequently had to adjust to living conditions that were very different from those they had enjoyed in Cuba. Here, Pedro Oliver, who had been the rector of a Cuban university, fixes a meal of canned food in the small hotel room where he lived in Miami in 1960.

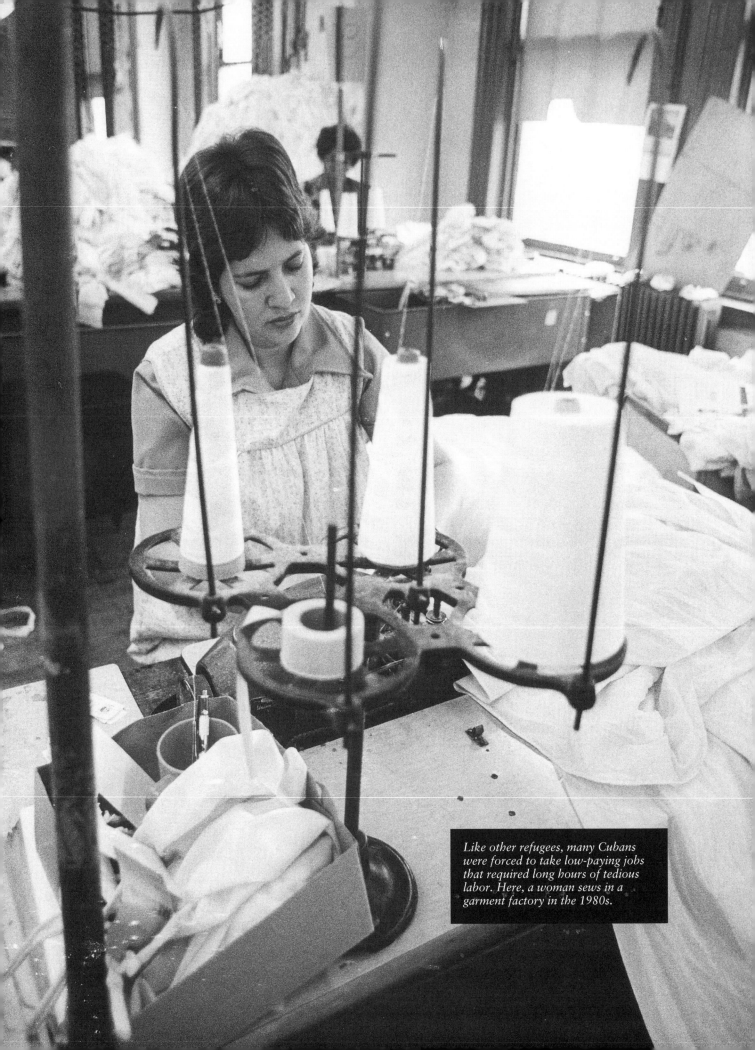

Like other refugees, many Cubans were forced to take low-paying jobs that required long hours of tedious labor. Here, a woman sews in a garment factory in the 1980s.

CHAPTER FOUR

A NEW LIFE

n 1869, a Spanish-born Cuban, Vincente Martínez Ybor, went to Key West, Florida, to start a cigar factory. Ybor had been a successful cigar manufacturer in Havana, but a high tariff on cigars had kept him from selling his products in the United States. Ybor realized that he could avoid the tariff by importing Cuban tobacco and producing "American-made" cigars in Florida.

There had been earlier cigar factories in Key West and New York City; these usually used tobacco grown in Florida. But Ybor devised more efficient ways of producing cigars and knew that smokers preferred the finer tobacco leaf grown in Cuba. Other Cuban manufacturers followed Ybor's lead in establishing Florida factories, and by the mid-1870s, Key West had 45 factories producing 25 million cigars every year. Ybor initiated a ferry service that ran from Havana to Key West three times a week.

Most of these factories were staffed by Cuban immigrants, who retained a custom they had enjoyed in Cuba. The workers hired a *lector* (reader) who sat on a *tribuna* (platform) in the middle of the workroom and read aloud from books and magazines that were also chosen by the workers. These readings were not just for entertainment, but for education as well. In addition to popular novels, the *lectors* read newspapers and political works, including those of socialists such as Karl Marx.

As a result, Cuban American cigar makers had a high level of political awareness. They were among the strongest supporters of the Cuban rebellions of 1868 and 1895. José Martí, who collected funds for his revolutionary party in the United States, called the readers' *tribunas* "pulpits of freedom." Vincente Martínez Ybor himself supported the Cuban independence movement.

Ybor was not as sympathetic, however, to the demands of his workers for higher pay. In the 1870s and 1880s, strikes frequently halted work in the Key West cigar factories. In addition, Key West's small size and isolation (until 1912 it could be reached only by sea) limited the growth of the cigar industry there. Ybor began to look for another site for his business.

In 1885, he and Ignacio Haya, a New York–based Cuban cigar maker, acquired 40 acres of swampland northeast of the town of Tampa, on Florida's Gulf Coast. Renamed Ybor City, this plot of land became a planned industrial community within a year. Streets were laid out in a grid pattern. Multistory factories arose, with Spanish-style wrought-iron balconies. Dozens of cottages were built to house the workers and their families.

By the spring of 1886, Ybor's factory was ready to produce its first cigars. Ironically, however, the Cuban workers went out on strike because Ybor had hired a Spanish bookkeeper. The honor of making the first cigar in Ybor City went to the factory of his partner from New York.

From the 1880s through the 1920s, Ybor City was known as "cigar city," attracting thousands of workers from Cuba, Spain, and Italy. Related industries, such as box factories and lithographic studios that turned out the colorful cigar labels, provided additional work. Some women worked in the cigar factories, and many others found work running boardinghouses or working in tailor shops, laundries, and grocery stores in Ybor City.

The growth of Florida's tourist industry in the early decades of the 20th century provided an additional source of employment for Cuban immigrants. Some worked in service jobs. Others participated in the construction of hotels and grand homes. Cuban-born architects, craftspeople, and construction workers helped create Spanish-style buildings in the city of Miami and nearby communities such as Coral Gables. From the 1920s onward, other Cubans arrived as agricultural laborers, harvesting sugar cane, avocados, and other tropical fruits.

The "golden exiles" who fled Fidel Castro's revolutionary government between 1959 and 1962 were probably the best-educated and wealthiest large group of immigrants ever to arrive in the United States. Many had been doctors, lawyers, bankers, business owners, and college professors in Cuba. Some found opportunities to use their skills in the United States.

But others had to take menial jobs far below their abilities. Most wealthy Cubans had to abandon their savings and property when they fled. Lawyers and doctors were not licensed to practice in the United States. Former teachers and engineers had to take jobs as garment workers, janitors, or maids. The language barrier also kept Spanish-speaking Cubans from finding well-paid jobs in the United States. A survey taken in the early 1970s showed that only 16 percent of refugees who had been lawyers in Cuba were able to practice their profession in the United States.

Nonetheless, there were countless success stories among the "golden exiles" and those that have followed since. Through sheer hard work and thrift, Cuban refugees prospered in their new surroundings. Carlos J. Arboleya, who had been a bank auditor in Cuba, arrived in Miami in 1960 with his wife and son and $40. He took a job as a shoe factory clerk. After hours, he studied the process of making shoes. Within a year and a half, Arboleya was made

Before 1960, the largest Cuban American community was in New York City. This Cuban business association in New York, called the Young Men of Tomorrow, bestows awards on a group of students in 1956.

vice-president of the company. But in 1962 he resigned to take a lower-paying but promising job in a bank. Six years later, he was president of Miami's Fidelity National Bank.

Arboleya told an interviewer in 1973 that his story was not unique. "You know, people come in on these airlifts and...they work two or three jobs. The wife works, everybody works.... Almost every day one of them walks into this

office...and says, 'Look—I've saved up $10,000 or $15,000. I want to deposit it in your bank and you to help me find a business to buy or start.'"

Indeed, the refugees became known for their entrepreneurial spirit. "Little Havana," the Miami neighborhood where many refugees settled, blossomed with Cuban-owned stores and restaurants. By 1973, Cuban Americans owned and operated more than 7,000 businesses in Miami and surrounding Dade County. Today, the figure is over 25,000, and Cuban Americans are found in the upper management of banks, insurance companies, and virtually every kind of business in the metropolitan area.

Among the many Cuban American-owned enterprises are construction companies, auto dealerships, radio and television stations, theaters, fishing fleets, and factories that produce shoes, garments, and other products. In the four decades since the first refugees from Castro's Cuba arrived, Miami has become a financial and trade center with links to every Latin American country. The ability to speak Spanish is no longer a bar to employment—it is almost a necessity.

Cuban Americans have as a whole achieved greater success in a shorter time than any comparable immigrant group in the history of the United States. A survey taken in the early 1990s indicated that about 18 percent of Cuban Americans held management jobs or were professionals such as doctors, lawyers, and teachers. By comparison, only about 15 percent of non-Hispanic whites occupied such positions. The number of Cuban Americans in technical, sales, and administrative support jobs was about 50 percent greater than for non-Hispanic whites. The same survey showed that about 25 percent of Cuban American households had incomes over $50,000, compared to about 18 percent of non-Hispanic white households.

Yet it would be wrong to conclude that all Cuban Americans have achieved economic success. As of 1990, about 20 percent of Cuban American households had incomes below $13,000. A study made in 1994 by the Cuban American National Council showed that the socioeconomic status of Cuban Americans was lower than that of non-Hispanic whites and of Asian Americans.

Like other immigrants, Cuban Americans have experienced many kinds of prejudice in their adopted land. Some of the 19th-century cigar workers in Florida were Cubans of African descent. They found that the state's discriminatory "Jim Crow" laws required blacks to take second place to whites in public accommodations and transportation, theaters, and schools.

Until very recently, Cuban American children of all races found that the textbooks and teachers in U.S. schools downplayed or ignored the Spanish contributions to the culture of the United States.

Nearly all Cuban immigrants have been Roman Catholics. Until the 1960s, particularly in the Protestant-dominated southern United States, they were therefore subject

Restaurants in Cuban American communities served familiar dishes, such as the Cuban sandwiches being made by this man in Tampa. A line of people indicates the popularity of his small takeout business.

to religious prejudice. Protestant missionaries went to Key West and Tampa to "save" Cuban immigrants from their "superstitions." (The missionaries had little success.)

Like all Spanish-speaking immigrants, Cubans have found an entrenched hostility toward those who do not speak English. The arrival of large numbers of Cuban refugees after 1959 has in some ways heightened these prejudices. Particularly in Miami and the other communities of Dade County, Florida, some Anglos became alarmed over the growth of the Cuban population.

Nevertheless, in 1973, the Dade County commissioners passed an ordinance that created a bilingual policy for the county. Traffic signs, offices in public buildings, election ballots, and public schools were required to use both Spanish and English. At the time, this seemed a reasonable response to the presence of so many Spanish-speaking residents.

But in 1980, the year of the Mariel boatlift, the county's voters repealed the ordinance after a divisive and emotional campaign. Eight years later, Floridians overwhelmingly approved a referendum to add an "English Only" amendment to the state constitution.

Sensational and distorted accounts in the media about the Mariel boatlift refugees tended to reflect badly on all Cuban immigrants. In 1982, a nationwide poll asked people if they thought the arrival of various ethnic groups had been good or bad for the country. More than half of the respondents thought that English, Irish, Jewish, German, Italian, and Polish immigrants had been "good," and more than 40 percent regarded Japanese, African, and Chinese immigrants as "good." But only 9 percent of those polled thought that Cubans had been "good" for the country.

THE CIGAR INDUSTRY

Domingo Ginestra was born in the town of Guanabacoa in Havana Province in 1865. His father was a cigar maker and Domingo followed in his footsteps, coming to Key West in 1886. In 1893, he left for Tampa and Ybor City. He described his experiences in the cigar industry to an interviewer in the 1930s.

Many are the hardships through which I have gone, but none like the different strikes that arose here from time to time. The first strike of importance was one that lasted seven months. It was called the "Weight Strike." It had been the custom of the manufacturers to weigh out 8 or 9 ounces of filler tobacco, and the workers had to produce fifty cigars from this amount. It was practically impossible to produce the required number with this amount, so we went on strike to eliminate the weighing of the material.

After this there came another strike that lasted seven months. This strike was called in order to have an increase in price and in order that a Regulation Committee be appointed. However, whenever we gained an increase of $1.00, the cost of living went up $2.00 so we were always the losers.

Still another strike was called in the year 1920, and which lasted ten months. During this strike we put up a sort of restaurant owned by all the workers. All the cigar-makers on strike were fed here, or food carried to their homes. By means of this joint ownership we could carry on the strike better. However, the manufacturers made some combination with the authorities with the result that one day a few policemen came to this place, destroying everything they could lay their hands on. The food, already cooked, and all the groceries were thrown out on the street.

The lector or reader was a highly respected and well-paid member of the cigar industry until 1931. Abelardo Gutiérrez Díaz arrived in Tampa from Cuba in the 1920s. He was born in Spain but emigrated to Cuba, and on the island he learned the skills of a lector. In an interview in 1974, he described his work.

We had four daily shifts (*turnos*). One was used to read national news stories. Another was devoted to international political developments. The third concerned itself entirely with news from the proletarian [working-class] press.... [Afterwards], we read news from Cuban dailies, such as *Diario de la Marina*. Cuban newspapers arrived in Tampa regularly throughout this period.

In the morning the day's reading started with national news, usually Spanish translations of the English-language

The first Cuban American cigar factories were established in Key West, Florida, in the early 19th century. This is the Estrela Cigar Company and some of its employees around 1920.

After Vincent Ybor built the first cigar factory in the Tampa area, the city became the leading producer of cigars in the United States. Tampa proudly displays its most famous product at a fair in 1908.

press.... And, of course, regardless of the *lector's* personal feeling, one simply could not read what he wanted. One was paid to read materials demanded by the cigar workers, not judge them.

And then the novel. The novel was also chosen by the cigar workers. There was a vote. Four or five novels by different authors would be submitted to a vote; the novel winning the largest number of votes determined the book selected for the *lectura*. The novel was read in installments, some twenty or thirty minutes per daily session. Every day a section would be read until the novel was completed. At that time, another election would determine the next novel.

Almost all the novels chosen were by Spanish authors.... [The French novelist Émile] Zola also enjoyed enormous popularity among the workers. At the beginning, almost all the novels involved serious themes, usually labor-related subjects— that was a time when the factories were made up almost entirely of men. Afterwards, during the late 1920s, women entered the factories in increasing numbers. And through the very force of the women's vote, we began to read more romantic novels and material treating the dashing adventurers....

Since one of the requirements necessary to become a *lector* involved literary skills, almost all *lectores* had received some form of formal education. But perhaps as important, one had to read with feeling (*leer con sentido*). More than anything else, one had to act out his material. Take the novel, for example. One had to interpret. The *lector* had to be something of

Cigars are still made in Tampa today. This man boxes Garcia y Vega cigars, one of the leading brands. Since imports of Cuban tobacco have been banned, the cigars are now made with leaves grown in the United States.

At this tobacco exhibit at the Florida State Fair in Tampa in 1941, the airplane and one woman's dress and boots are made entirely of cigars.

an actor. He had to breathe life into his protagonists. The old lady—the old man: when they argued, when they yelled. All that. You know, it was not all that easy.

And quite naturally, there were favorite *lectores*. Some *lectores* were sought after more than others. There was often competition among factories to secure the service of a particularly gifted *lector*. Those who had the theatrical flair, who portrayed the protagonists with style and drama—these men were typically the most popular. There was one case of a *lector* who did not have a powerful voice, but who was a tremendous performer. He was an artist—today he would have been a film star.

And there were difficulties and bad times. Because we read and disseminated the labor press, we incurred the hostility of the factory owners. We were accused of making communist propaganda. That simply was not true. The cigar workers paid, and one had to read precisely what the cigar workers wanted. Management did not approve of this system. It was [at] the height of one of these controversies that they abolished the *lectura*. They removed the platform on which we sat. At this point, the workers took to the streets. The mayor personally inquired into the nature of the problem. We informed him we wanted the *lectura* restored. We were informed that management would reinstate the *lectura* only if the material read to the workers was approved beforehand by the owners. And naturally, since it was not the factory owners who paid out wages—it was the factory workers—we could not accept; similarly, the workers rejected a system in which management se-

In most cigar factories, the employees hired a lector to read to them as they worked. Sitting on a platform, he read aloud from newspapers and books. The most popular lectors provided education as well as entertainment.

lected the materials presented. The *lectura* ended in 1931. After the strike, many *lectores* returned to the factories as cigar workers. And I, with a compatriot, opened up a little café in Ybor.

Many women worked in the cigar factories. Dolores Rio was born in 1909 in West Tampa. She started working in a cigar factory in 1923 and retired in 1974, after 51 years—the first cigar worker in Tampa to receive a pension.

I went to the factory, Sanchez y Haya. I was fourteen years old when I started then. I went over there to learn to make cigars, and I was working with someone teaching me, helping me. But in two weeks, the old man who was the foreman there (I think he liked me or something, he always called me "Lolita"), he says, "You're going to earn money." My father worked there and my aunt, so he says, "How would you like to learn bunches? You make bunches and your aunt rolls." I say okay, if you want, I'll do it. So the first paycheck, I got, I never forget—$3.25. I went "AYYY," and I took it home to my mother. Then the old man says, "Do you want to learn to work by hand?" I say yes, I want to learn. So he says, "Go to your father in the afternoon." So I used to go and make by hand bunches for my father so he can make more cigars. Then one day, I was so scared, but I didn't say no. He says. "Hey, I'm going to make you a bunchmaker. You're going to make bunches for two rollers." It's different making for two. Every time they finish one more, you got to have another ready....

Q: *Were there more Cuban women who became bunchmakers and rollers?*

Rio: Way back, at the beginning, it was only men. Then they start like they do now. They don't want the women. The only thing the woman could do in the factory was to strip the tobacco leaves. Italian women were strippers too. Italian, Cuban, Spanish, they all try to get on as rollers because they all want to make more money....

Q: *Do you remember any strikes during your first years in the factory?*

Rio: Yes, they were going to start holding our paychecks back one week, they said. We went on strike, we don't want it. Then they say okay, how about just two days, so we say okay and go back. Of course, then later they go to three days and four, and finally they get their week anyways.

Q: *Did you make a lot less money during the Depression?*

Rio: Oh yes, everyone was making less. We were on a limit. You know it's piece work, but they put you on limit. We only work three days or whatever. They keep on working, but they earn less. But it's better to earn less than to be in the streets.

Paulina Pedroso

The early Cuban communities in the United States were devoted to the cause of freedom for their homeland. José Martí called the Cuban neighborhoods in Tampa the "civilian camps of the revolution." Paulina Pedroso, a Cuban-born woman of African descent, was one of those who joined the struggle.

After the defeat of the Cuban rebels in the Ten Years' War, Paulina and her husband, Ruperto, left Cuba for Key West. Sometime in the 1880s they moved to the brand-new community of Ybor City, outside Tampa. Ruperto got a job in the cigar industry, and Paulina ran a boardinghouse. Her establishment on 12th Street and Eighth Avenue catered to the many young single men working in the cigar business.

Paulina's most famous guest would be José Martí himself. On a train trip to Florida, he fell ill from exhaustion and she nursed him back to health. After Martí had been the target of an assassination attempt, Ruperto slept in front of the door of Martí's room as a guard.

It became Martí's custom to stay with the Pedrosos whenever he went to Tampa. Paulina flew the Cuban flag outside as a signal that he was present, and crowds gathered to catch sight of Martí.

Paulina worked tirelessly for her people's welfare. The Pedrosos and their friends became the nucleus of an interracial coalition that joined the Cuban Revolutionary Party. In 1900, she helped to found an African-Cuban mutual aid society, La Unión Martí-Maceo, that still exists today.

When the fight for independence began in 1894, the Tampa community was generous in its support. When news of Martí's death reached Florida, the Pedrosos sold their house and gave the proceeds to the Cuban cause. They lived very simply afterward. In 1910, the couple returned to Cuba, where the government gave them a house to live in rent free. Paulina Pedroso died in 1913.

Today, on the lot in Ybor City where their home once stood, a plaque acknowledges Paulina's role. It reads: "Paulina Pedroso was one of the great woman patriots of Cuba."

La verbena del tabaco *means "the tobacco festival." The women shown here were the "queens" of such a festival in Tampa in 1935.*

During the Depression, the Works Progress Administration (WPA) sponsored a project to record the oral histories of many Americans. One WPA employee obtained this interview with a woman of Cuban descent.

I was born in Key West, Florida, in the year 1900. I am now 35 years of age, and have lived in the United States all my life. At the age of 22 years, I came to Ybor City with my husband and a little daughter of six years. My husband found work immediately and we lived for a while very happy and contented. Here I learned the trade of cigar-buncher and was, therefore, able to help my husband in...covering the expenses of our growing family. We had seven children.

Last year, however, my husband lost his position as cigar-maker and he abandoned me and the seven children. For a time I continued at my work as buncher, and although I did not make enough to keep my children in clothing, I was able to feed them properly. However, more and more machines were introduced into the cigar factory, until I also lost my position. Since then I have not been able to find work at anything.

My daughter, who was born in Key West, and is not [yet] 19 years of age was able to obtain work at the FERA [Federal Emergency Relief Agency] making dresses. She works only one day a week for which she is paid $8.00 a month or $2.00 per week. Outside of this little sum, I have no other means of support for myself and children.

As can be imagined I was only barely able to pay the rent with this sum, so I [started] to sell a few of my furniture every time I found myself hard up for money. Now I have practically nothing left in the house, but a bed into which we all try to huddle at night. Since all my furniture has given out, I have had to take the $2.00 a week that my daughter makes in order to buy groceries. I have had to neglect my rent, and I am afraid that soon I will be thrown out of the house. If this happens, where can I go? I have no relatives or friends to whom I can go in this extremity. If I was alone I could readily find a room with some charitable friend, but with such a large family I cannot do this. There are many days in which I feed my children but my daughter and myself go hungry. I am, therefore, in a desperate condition.

I have been receiving letters from my step-sister, who left for New York some time ago, and she tells me to go there by all means, as I can find work there. I am, therefore, leaving this coming week with all my children as I believe that I will be in a better position there to support my family since I cannot look forward to any help from my husband. I do not know where he is or whether he is living or dead.

I would gladly remain here if I could get my former position as cigar buncher, or for that matter any other form of employment.

José Yglesias grew up in Ybor City in the 1920s and 1930s. He wrote in 1977 about the effects of global political events on the cigar makers.

The Depression hit a luxury industry like Ybor City's hard, and the new generations were being weaned away. With the second World War the industry rallied, and it did well, too, in the postwar years. Although the readers were no longer in the factories, there was still political struggle; during the Spanish Civil War the town was almost, one might say, on a war footing to help the Republic. In the postwar period, the factory owners did finally negotiate with their CIO [Congress of Industrial Organizations] representatives, but in the days of Joe McCarthy [a Wisconsin senator noted for his investigations of communists] the radical leaders were blacklisted—nothing new for Ybor City: there had always been blacklists after a strike.

The final blow came with the revolution in Cuba. You could not make first-rate cigars without tobacco from the Vuelta Abajo area of Pinar del Rio. That's that. And our embargo cut if off. Most Latins in Ybor City were *fidelistas*, and they did not hold it against "*el caballo*" [the horse] that the end had come. For the old-timers the embargo was further proof of the barbarity of *americanos*—the "crackers" with hair on their teeth who once broke up their union meetings and called them "Cuban niggers." The new Cuban exiles were for them new indeed—they were counter-revolutionary.

Today, cigar factories operate in Miami's Little Havana. Rolling the cigars by hand into just the right thickness and tightness requires skill and experience. Smokers regard machine-rolled cigars as inferior.

LOOKING FOR A JOB

Carlos Garcia came to the United States in 1946 "looking for a better way of living" because jobs were scarce in Cuba. He spoke with an interviewer in 1989.

Like everybody else, I spoke very little English, but I always have been a very ambitious man. Hard-working, but ambitious. I think the world, in any kind of political system, needs ambitious people. In any kind of system, if you don't work you don't have. This we have to learn, especially in socialist countries. You must work and work hard and be productive and work good or you're not going to get nothing. So, I worked hard. Then I became a busboy because there was always the tips, you know, and then I became a waiter. And I was room-service waiter and I was a cocktail waiter—all kinds of waiters I have been. I tumbled around for the first couple of years.... I started to work in the Sherry Netherlands [a large hotel in New York City] in 1948 as a busboy and on room service and I met the most exciting people in the world. Ernest Hemingway, Mickey Rooney, Cary Grant, Gary Cooper—everybody in the movies, in business.

Teresita de Blank, the daughter of wealthy sugar planters, left Cuba after the Castro revolution. She described the difficulties many exiles experienced finding work in the United States.

You have to remember that when we first came to this country, our most profound experience was probably that of seeing at close quarters our parents' terrible frustrations. Fathers who had been immensely successful back in Cuba ended up sitting around the house—the extremely modest house, I need hardly add—sometimes literally for years on end. These self-sufficient, proud men found themselves dependent on their wives for their families' survival, and you can imagine the effect that had on them. And, of course, among the younger generation, there were so many who became distraught at seeing their world turned upside down. All they wanted was to get married, to be taken care of, and to find a new cocoon in which to live.

Rodolfo de León came to the United States in 1962 with his mother and brother. His father, who had his own business in Cuba, followed a year later.

Seeing my mother was depressing. She was trying to get work. I remember she finally found work before my father came, for maybe four, five, or six months. She was working in a *camaronera*, shrimp-packing, to get the thing out of the shrimp to be packed. Her fingers, a piece of her

During the Great Depression years of the 1930s, this Florida man earned a living picking coconuts and taking them into the city to sell.

This lunch-counter cook in West Palm Beach, Florida, works in front of a mural depicting popular entertainment figures. Pollo campero means "chickens that have been allowed to run free"—just as the best-tasting chickens were in Cuba.

hand is wasted, you can see it—take a look at her hand. It's from peeling shrimps. She probably came home with $30 after about forty, forty-five hours. She came home at five, maybe six o'clock.

My father couldn't find work, couldn't find work. When he did, he found it in Boca Raton, sixty miles away from Miami. He picked tomatoes. And that was sixty miles away. They had a car pool, and some guy took him. So he had to pay, I don't know how much. He went about five o'clock in the morning and came back about ten o'clock at night. He got paid six dollars a day. [He paid] two dollars for the car, something like that.

Many Cuban professionals could not practice in the United States. Moreover, for many the only thought was to make money immediately to bring more members of the family to the United States. Irma de Leon, who was a judge in Cuba, fled in 1962 at the age of 48 with her daughter. She wanted to make money so that she could help her husband get out.

The first thing I did in Miami was taking care of little children. This was something very new for me. Because in Cuba we have no babysitters. In Cuba, all the relatives—the grandmothers and the aunts and the older sisters—take care of the children, but here it is another business. When that was not enough, I started cleaning houses one day a week, and so after one of the ladies wanted me to be a steady maid and I decided to do that. She was paying $35 a week, which I felt was a great deal of money. I needed $400 to bring my husband from Cuba, so I said, "Oh this is great." It was the first time that I started working with a vacuum

Many women in exiled Cuban families took jobs outside the home. Though this violated tradition, it was necessary in order to earn enough money to support their families.

cleaner...oh...[laughs], the first day that I cleaned all the house, my back was killing me! When I came home I told my daughter, "Please, take my shoes, because I can't move, and today you have to warm some canned soup or something, because I can't cook."

I was adjusting little by little to the work in that home. I cooked the lunch for them and ironed, washed the clothes and everything. I was real happy with that job, very, very happy. Yes, I was a lawyer, a judge, in Cuba, but here I couldn't do that and so I was very fortunate that I could work and earn money. I have no hard feelings....

Later, the lady I worked for was moving back to Washington or something, so I started working in a factory, sewing, because I loved to sew. The problem was I did not have experience with factory machines. The first day that I started working there, I pushed the pedal and the machine went backwards and the lady was asking me, "You know about this?" And I said, "Yes, I have some experience." But when she saw me, oh dear! But no, she gave me the job. That work was really something because I had to work eight hours sitting, and I couldn't even look around because I was not as fast as they ask and I couldn't make the minimum.

Pedro Reboredo came to the United States in 1962 after a short stay in Venezuela. He was 19 years old and had almost no money. Later, he would become an engineer and the mayor of West Miami. On his arrival, he stayed with a friend, Ramón Ferrer.

Ramón let me stay at his family's house in Fort Lauderdale, around thirty miles north of Miami, and he found me a job at the Governor's Club Hotel. I started out as a busboy. Though it was a step above washing dishes, it was a difficult experience. Though I had studied some English at school in Cuba, my ability to speak or comprehend the language was very poor. And I was eager to do things right.

My first day at the restaurant, I tried so hard that I attempted to carry a pile of the most expensive dishes. I broke around twelve of them. The hostess made fun of me by saying all kinds of silly things in English that I couldn't understand: "You dumb Cubans are good for nothing." I kept saying, "Yes, yes." I didn't understand her. But I was so nervous, and I wanted to please her. My friend was standing next to her, laughing his head off.

But the people at the hotel were very nice. Newly arrived Cubans had such a warm reception from Americans in South Florida, we felt like we were at home. Although we thought a lot about our families, who were still in Cuba.

Language difficulties often limited the types of jobs available to Cuban immigrants. Felisa Colon, a Chinese Cuban, was 22 when she came to New York City in the 1960s.

My uncle paid my school for three months to learn English, and as a way of practicing, I used to go places and ask for things. One day I went for a job, and I got the job—I couldn't believe it! I was just practicing. They gave me a secretarial position in a bank audit department, and I was just practicing. Then I got there and found that I couldn't do it. The telephone rang and I started to cry because I didn't know how to answer the telephone. My boss comes out, he's a very nice man—"Felisa, why don't you answer the telephone?" And I don't know what to say—"Mr. Ryan, because nobody is going to call me!" I was crying and I felt really really bad and I said, "I want to quit. I don't know English." He was nice enough to transfer me to a typing pool, and there I picked up a lot of English. And when I knew enough, I went to an insurance company, and that's how I started working in personnel. And later I changed to a subsidiary company, where I'm still working.

Gisela Feil came to Fort Wayne, Indiana, in 1962. She described her first job.

The first job I had in the United States was folding diapers at the Troy Laundry, which I appreciated very much. You don't need English for that, just numbers: *uno, dos, tres....* I was there for a year and later worked for Lincoln Life. By then my English was better and I could work at a translating job. When my father arrived, I found him a job in the supply department of the same insurance company where I worked. My mother had always been a seamstress— she took this training in Europe [she was originally from Romania]—so when she came here, she was able to work as a seamstress at home.

At first, it was necessary for everyone in the family to work if they were to recover their middle-class status in the new country. Yet many Cuban women kept their jobs after they were no longer essential for the economic well-being of their families. Sociologist Yolanda Prieto interviewed Cuban immigrant women in Hudson County, New Jersey, in 1990. She spoke to a 40-year-old woman who had graduated from college in Cuba.

I am an elementary school teacher. Even though my husband has a business now I want to continue working. I think it would be inconsiderate on my part to stay home while he works. Life is very expensive and we Cubans are used to living comfortably.... No wonder most Cuban women have jobs here. Cuban women have been forced to help their families recuperate in only a few years the standard of living they had achieved in Cuba before communism took over.

Sewing was a traditional skill for women in Cuba, and it helped this woman find work in a New York City garment factory.

BUSINESS AND CAREER

Gustavo Pérez Firmat came to Miami in 1960. He described Little Havana *in his memoir* Next Year in Cuba.

During the 1960s and 1970s Calle Ocho, or Eighth Street, was a busy, bustling one-way thoroughfare lined with restaurants, supermarkets, gas stations, bakeries, florists, fruit stands, barbershops, car dealerships, furniture showrooms, appliance stores, *botánicas* [stores for religious artifacts used in Afro-Cuban rituals], funeral parlors, and schools. Anything one needed could be found on Calle Ocho, which was located in the heart of Little Havana. As sociologists put it, the community that sprang up around this street was institutionally complete. An individual who lived there could be delivered by a Cuban obstetrician, buried by a Cuban undertaker, and in between birth and death lead a perfectly satisfactory life without needing extramural contacts. Little Havana was a golden cage, an artificial paradise, the neighborhood of dreams.

Many of the establishments on Calle Ocho were *mami*-and-*papi* stores that supported and employed a whole family. While the grandmother stayed home with the small children, Mami and Papi worked the store. Once the children were old enough, they too came to work after school and on Saturday

In the years before the refugees from Castro's Cuba arrived, Cuban Americans frequently traveled back and forth from the United States to their homeland. This travel agency in Key West in the late 1940s offered a half-hour plane trip to Havana for only $10.

mornings. Some of the businesses in Little Havana had not existed in Havana, but others had been re-created in their Cuban image.

Shortly after the arrival of the Marielito refugees, Sergio Pereira, a Cuban American county manager, commented on their importance in the development of the Cuban community in Miami.

Cubans have, for the past two decades, made a tremendous contribution to Dade County. We all know the success stories of Cuban lawyers and bankers. Indeed, commercial liaisons with Latin American clients and land development ventures have established Cubans as economic leaders. With the passing of time, upward mobility has created openings at the semiskilled levels. Now the labor force is suddenly here to fill the gap. Of course, the new arrivals will need time to retrain, to adjust to life in an environment of abundance and freedom.... So they, and therefore we in this community are now in a state of flux. History shows us that this too will pass and that we are on our way to greater prosperity.

Mike Yip is a Cuban American of Chinese descent. Today he is manager and part-owner of La Caridad, a very popular Cuban-Chinese restaurant on the Upper West Side of New York City. He revealed the secret of his success.

Before I left Cuba in 1969, my father told me to save some money. If I earned some money, don't spend all of it. You make ten dollars, try to save half. That's the only way you'll change. That's the only way you can get whatever you want in the future. That's true. And people don't

Union City, New Jersey, is today the second-largest center of Cuban American life. This meat market is one of the many Cuban-owned businesses on Bergenline Avenue, the main street of Union City.

like to save…because there are so many things that they want to buy. But if you save, in a year if you want something you'll have it. That's the only way you're going to do better….

When I came to New York, I lived with my godfather, who had already come from Cuba. I went to school for two years, and worked part-time after school. I began to save some money.

After that, I was 16 and it was hard to continue going to school and working at the same time. I decided to work, save some money, and bring my parents and sister over.

I started working for my uncle in his restaurant. That was a smaller restaurant not far from here. Then, the Cuban-Chinese family who owned this one sold it to him, and he took over. That was 25 years ago. I have been working here almost 18 years. We have a long-term lease, but when it expires, I don't know if we'll stay here.

The Chinese dishes are old Cantonese style. The Chinese people who came to Cuba were mostly from Canton province. They began to open Chinese restaurants in Cuba, they served fried rice, chop suey, chow mein, food like that. And then they thought about it, and said, you know people here in Cuba eat different food. We could make that too. So they started Cuban cooking. So if you and your wife go out and you say, "I feel like having some Chinese food today," and she says, "I want Cuban food," you can come here. You can have some of both.

So after we took over this restaurant, we changed things. Before, it had mostly Cuban customers who liked the food spiced a certain way. American people like it less salty, a little different taste. What we did, we changed a lot of things to American style. We gave the customers whatever they liked. If a customer suggested something, we did it. We changed, and started doing better and better. Because we served what our customers liked.

Benita Nuñez came to the United States in 1970 and settled in Chicago. After working in a factory, she built her own business.

I had worked for Western Electric from 1970 to 1975 when I was laid off for the third time. I was tired of that, and I said "I don't like working where I don't have any security. I would like to learn something where if I lost my job, it's not so bad to find another one."… One of my sisters, the one that was a beautician also, she always told me, "Well, you like to cut hair—why don't you try it?" And I said, "Well, I don't know, let's try it." I like to face challenges. Somebody else did it; why can't I?

It was something that wasn't going to take me too long. So I gave my deposit to the school and I said, "I'm going to try it for a few weeks, and if I think I can make it, I'll stay; if not, I'll leave. If I lose my deposit it's fine." But thank God, I liked it, and I decided to stay….

In this business, you really don't have to put so much money. You don't invest really a lot of money because it's

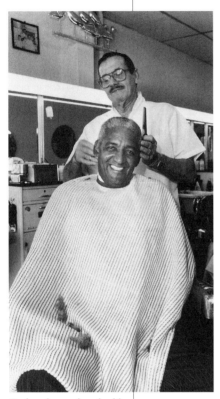

Barber shops often double as social centers in Cuban American communities. In this shop in Miami's Little Havana, the barber and his customer share a joke.

more like a service that you're giving. It's not like when you have a store and you have to put money in the merchandise. All you have to worry about is to pay the rent. You buy supplies according to the business you have. You have a lot of business, you buy more supplies and the telephone, electricity, and insurance. It's not like other businesses where you have to put a lot of money to start.

My husband encouraged me. He said, "Well, if you think you can do it, do it; you don't lose nothing trying." My husband didn't look at it that I was stronger than he was because he wasn't the one that was going into business. We tried to work together. Even now when we have the beauty shop, it's not only me that works there. My husband does the cleaning of the shop, helps me with the supplies, everything I need....

I've been very satisfied with what I have accomplished. I guess I showed something that I really could do, and I am happy with what I am doing.

Sofia Rodriguez was a school principal in Cuba and came to this country after the Castro revolution. She settled with her family in Bluffton, Indiana, where she resumed her role as an educator. She has been so successful that she was named Indiana Teacher of the Year. She expressed her feelings about the importance of education.

I am a born teacher, I think. I don't want to look bragging about this, but what I have found is that my love for kids and my love for people and my desire to live is so great that it was not difficult for me to adjust to American ways. It was not difficult because what you need to teach is really to feel inside the desire to give the best you can, the best you have, and to inspire the kids to give themselves the best they have.

I have received much more than I have given to my students. We understand each other, and they inspire me and I hope I inspire them. It's a learning situation and it is the giving and taking that makes a real nice atmosphere for students to learn the language. I also have the dream, that they understand the Hispanic culture better and through foreign languages become better citizens, better Americans, and better educated about the differences in the world....

Today I value education more than ever. We lost everything we possessed in Cuba, but the one thing that Castro could never take away from us was our education. It has been the main factor to succeed in this country.

Belkis Musalen came to the United States from Cuba in the early 1960s as a very young child. She described how she chose her career.

I chose dentistry as my career because it kind of incorporated everything that I enjoyed. I enjoy working with my hands. I love being with people, and I've always had an interest in health care, especially working with children.

You can use dentistry in so many ways, it's incredible. You don't have to have a practice, the little white house with the

Julio Bulnes, shown here with his wife and daughter, operates a successful photography business in Union City, New Jersey. Behind them is a display of his photos of weddings, baptisms, and quinceañeras *(a girl's 15th birthday celebration)—three important events in every Cuban American community.*

Today, many Cuban American women have become successful in business. Cary de Leon, president of Miami's Latin Business and ProfessionalWomen's Club in the late 1980s, is a Cuban American.

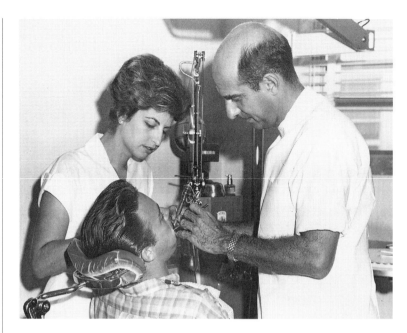

Many of the post-1960 Cuban refugees were professionals, trained in medicine, dentistry, and law. To resume their careers in the United States, they had to pass licensing examinations in an unfamiliar language. Yet most, like this dentist in Miami, eventually succeeded.

picket fence with the shingle outside; you can work in a hospital with children or do it part-time in the event you have a family.

Dentistry is a very expensive career to go into. Not only is it expensive to go through school but by the time you finish, most people are so in debt that they can't open up their own practice. And then by the time you get a building, equipment, one or two people to start off with, you can count on having to borrow about $100,000. I have no plans to start a practice....

One of my professors in dental school is Dr. Nereyda Clark, also a Cuban. She's my role model because she looks at dentistry as a service. She's one of the most active professors, as far as community things. She helped me to organize a health expo at a local mall, where we screened 208 people for oral cancer. It was a free service and it was a lot of work, but she was there because she cares and sees it as a service, not as a status quo thing. That's why I am in it.

Salvador Longoria came to the United States with his family in 1962, when he was four years old. Longoria was honored by the Louisiana State Bar Association as Outstanding Young Lawyer of 1991.

Once I mastered English, I enjoyed school and became a good student. While attending undergraduate courses at Loyola University, I decided that my mission in life was to learn public interest law and work with the Hispanic community and the disenfranchised.

Confronted with economic reality when I graduated from law school in 1983, I willingly accepted an offer to join the prestigious firm of Fawer, Brian, Hardy, and Zatzkis. I was involved primarily in litigation of state and federal criminal defense cases, and appellate work, as well as personal injury and tort suits. It was an excellent learning experience, and I remained with the company for three years. But in 1986 I chose to return to my original commitment to aid an under-represented segment of the community. With Michele Gaudin, I formed the partnership of Gaudin and Longoria. We handled all types of civil, criminal, and administrative cases, including litigation and consultation. At first it was a monetary setback, and I was forced to move back with my parents. However, the outcome proved worthwhile, and I am delighted that over 60 percent of my clientele are Hispanic. Moreover, I am supervising attorney of a clinical project at Tulane Law School. The program was established to work with Cubans who migrated to the United States as part of the Mariel flotilla and are incarcerated as a result of a felony conviction. The project provides legal representation to those who wish to appeal deportation. While [I'm] on the subject of Marielitos imprisoned in Louisiana, I served as mediating attorney at the Cuban prisoner uprising in Oakdale in 1987.

Dr. Rosa Vazquez, a child psychologist, believes that her father's role as an advisor in their home village influenced her career choice as well as her brother's; he became a psychiatrist. She described an experience she had here that highlighted her identity as a Cuban American.

I was in the middle of a family therapy workshop, and we were using a technique called sculpting. In this technique, the subject takes other people in the room (we were doing it with our classmates), and arranges them. You have to pick up [others who represent] your family and put them in certain poses. I volunteered: Oh, I'm going to do my family. Great family. I love my family. We were told to pick a point in your childhood that was significant for you. I had no idea what I was going to do. No idea whatsoever. And I put a man with one foot in one place and one foot in another, looking forward. I put the woman looking back, with one foot forward. I put the man representing my brother in the middle with the most puzzled face in the world and looking at both of them. And I put the woman representing myself in the middle of this triangle, mom dad and my brother, looking at all of them and looking back. They were supposed to ask all these people how they feel when they were doing this. And when they asked the woman who represented me how she felt, I started crying and crying. Very embarrassing, in the middle of a training class. Crying like a baby. And they asked me, what did you depict there? I said, "That's the day we left Cuba." It was very powerful. I must have been, already 27 or 28. In other words, I had been out of Cuba for a long time. I had never thought about all of this. I did not remember in my analysis about leaving Cuba. And this is what I come up with. Of course, the next day I went to my analyst and I said, "This is like somebody opened a faucet. And things are coming out. I'm having memories of my grandparents. Of the woman who took care of me. Of my toys. Of the smells of my house, of my bedroom." And I was crying and crying in my therapy. Sad, because I had left that.... I went through it again, symbolically, in therapy. I didn't know it would be so traumatic!

Miami's Little Havana today attracts tourists searching for authentic Cuban American food. The woman shown here offers a special on camarones empanizados (breaded, fried shrimp).

PREJUDICE

The Cuban American novelist Cristina Garcia came to the United States in 1961, when she was two. Though she was accepted by the non-Latino children in her neighborhood, she resented the images of Latinos in American culture.

I knew I was different—not only because my home life had little to do with America but because I never saw anybody remotely resembling me or my family in anything I ever read, watched on television, or heard from my friends. Ricky Ricardo seemed like an oddity. More common [on television] were the gangsters, thieves, gardeners, junkies, Romeos, spitfires, and occasional maids always named Maria who announced, "Look, *we* are the Latinos in the United States."...

When I told people I was Cuban, I'd invariably get one of three responses. The first (and most common) was the least offensive: a good-natured imitation of rapid-fire, made-up Spanish punctuated by "*Caramba!*"

The second, "You don't *look* Cuban," made my scalp prickle. How was I supposed to respond? Was this their idea of a compliment? "So what am I supposed to look like?" I'd ask. Without hesitation, they'd often reply, "Well, you know...*dark.*" That last word was whispered, nose wrinkled, as if to say, "You can't really be one of *them.*"

The third (most ludicrous) response was, "Oh, you speak English so well!" "Thank you," I'd say, straight-faced. "I've been practicing since I was two and a half." Still, my sarcasm wouldn't register. They'd smile blankly, convinced they'd just done something good by encouraging me to become a full-fledged American.

Juliana Flores came to the United States with her husband in 1956. He died fighting during the attempted invasion of Cuba at the Bay of Pigs in 1961. She described the anti-Cuban prejudice she encountered in Miami.

As a whole I have met friendly and nice people through my life. I have met some people [with a bias] against Cubans.... I feel those people are against any person that is a threat to their security. I have seen and I have read in the Miami area many times that some people expressed themselves, "Oh, I don't like those Cubans," or they are complaining about what the Cubans have done and the change that they have brought to the Miami area. Some are very disgusted about that, and they have complained that they don't like Cubans. When they say that, I feel that I am included. I am friendly to everybody and try to be an example for Cubans so that I do not hear anymore "I don't like those Cubans."

Because the U.S. government suspected them of being criminals, many of the people in the Mariel boatlift were held in federal prisons for years without trials. Fearing they were about to be deported to Cuba, prisoners in the Atlanta prison rioted in 1987. Deysi Lopez, the wife of one of the inmates, wept outside the prison fence as she waited to hear what had happened to her husband.

The bad publicity surrounding the refugees in the Mariel boatlift intensified prejudice against all Cuban Americans, as Pedro Reboredo described.

The Mariel program backfired on the U.S. government and caused a lot of trouble for the Cuban-American community. A Communist defector estimated that, out of the 125,000 Mariel refugees, around three thousand were Castro's agents, besides the criminals and mental cases sent by Castro to make Cuban refugees look like bad people.

It's true that the previous waves of Cuban refugees were better educated and better accepted by Americans. But toward the late 1970s, even those Cubans were feeling friction. Local people began to feel that maybe we weren't adaptable. Perhaps we didn't break our ties to Cuba as fast as people who came to America from other countries. Then the Mariel people forced a more drastic separation between the Anglos and the Cubans. In response, people like myself said, "We have to demonstrate to our American neighbors that Castro's rule made these Marielitos what they are. And we have to show that Cuban Americans are just as American as anybody else. We love this country. Just because the bad among the Marielitos came here, other people shouldn't have to move away from Miami."

We became more involved in community affairs. Some people participated in the United Way and other charities to show the American people, "No matter what my last name is, I am American."

After the Castro revolution, Belkis Musalen and her family first settled in Boston, where they had relatives. There, being of Cuban descent meant being different.

Imagine yourself an immigrant child in a different country in a new community, attending a new school, and meeting new friends all tied together by a common culture and language different from your own native ones. With a few Cuban families in our town, it seemed that my sister and I were forever the only Cuban kids in our neighborhood...and she was even born in Boston! I grew to despise the word "refugee" with all of its connotations and associated stereotypes....

Then one day, while writing an essay on "Freedom" for a ninth-grade English class, I asked my parents for the details to the many stories I'd heard on why we left Cuba. This was a turning point in my life. It was not until then that I came to grips with who I was, where I was going with school, and where I stood in the community. I remember my mother confronting me with the question, "Aren't you proud of your family, your heritage, your roots?" As I choked for words, she proceeded to remind me of a truth that has never left my heart. She said, "You cannot deny your roots. They only grow deeper with time to bind you to those you love and those that love you."

Agustín Román

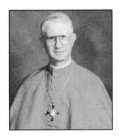

The refugees of the Mariel boatlift found a defender in the Most Reverend Agustín Román, auxiliary bishop of Miami. Born in 1928 in a rural area of the province of Havana, Román entered the seminary when he was 17. He was ordained into the priesthood in 1959, the year before Castro came to power. The revolutionaries regarded the Catholic Church as an enemy; Father Román was arrested in 1961 and was later expelled from Cuba.

Román arrived in the United States in February 1966, at a time when thousands of Cuban refugees were flocking to Miami. He knew that he had found his mission. He later wrote, "I understood then that here was where the Church needed me. I saw so many people who were exiled like sheep without a shepherd and realized that the diocese of Miami was struggling with more than it could handle."

The archbishop of Miami asked Román to supervise the construction of the Shrine of Our Lady of Charity. Our Lady of Charity was the patroness of Cuba and therefore a very important religious image for the Cuban exiles. By 1973 the shrine on Biscayne Bay was finished.

Consecrated a bishop in 1979, Román had the duty of overseeing the parishes in the archdiocese of Miami. His greatest challenge began with the Mariel boatlift. "In 1980 within a five-month period we experienced the exodus of 125,000 Cubans," Román recalled. "The Catholic Church welcomed them and it was the Church who tried to find those who were lost. They used to come for everything to the Church. For this reason when some of them suffered imprisonment in the United States they wanted the Church to come to their assistance."

In December 1986, rioting broke out among Marielitos in the federal prisons in Atlanta, Georgia, and Oakdale, Louisiana. Detained for years without charges being brought against them, they feared being deported to Cuba. The prisoners asked for Bishop Román to represent them. He negotiated an end to the crisis without bloodshed. When reporters called him a hero, Román responded with characteristic humility: "A bishop, a priest, is a servant, not a hero."

Frank G. and Esperanza B. de Varona celebrate Mother's Day with their grandchildren in Miami in 1991.

CHAPTER FIVE

PUTTING DOWN ROOTS

Calle Ocho! The name is Spanish for "Eighth Street," but in the early 1960s, Calle Ocho became the center of Cuban American life. In 1959, Eighth Street was part of a run-down low-rent district in Miami. Within the next 10 years, more than a quarter of a million Cuban refugees moved into the area, now called Little Havana. And Calle Ocho was the heart of it.

To newcomers, Calle Ocho seemed no different from a street in Cuba. Spanish was the universal language. Restaurants served Cuban sandwiches of cheese and ham, hearty plates of black beans and rice, chicken and shrimp with Cuban seasonings, and such familiar dishes as *ropa vieja* (literally "old clothes," which refers to shredded strips of stewed beef). Cuban immigrants could attend Spanish-language church services, listen to Spanish-language TV and radio stations, and read Spanish newspapers. Even the street signs of Little Havana were printed in Spanish.

Other U.S. cities also felt the influence of Cuban immigrants. The Union City area of Hudson County, New Jersey—just across the Hudson River from Manhattan—became home to the

second-largest Cuban American community. Cuban Americans operate metropolitan New York's Spanish-language TV station as well as many radio stations, newspapers, and magazines.

Chicago and Los Angeles saw the rise of sizable Cuban American populations after 1959, though there, as in other cities, Cuban Americans tended to live in integrated neighborhoods instead of all-Cuban enclaves.

Most of the Cuban refugees who arrived in the 1960s saw themselves as temporary exiles. Like other Cubans who had fled at different times during the 19th and early 20th centuries, they believed that they would return after the current Cuban government had fallen. And like those earlier exiles, the Castro-era refugees hoped to play a role in overthrowing that government.

During 1959 and 1960, the U.S. Central Intelligence Agency (CIA) financed and trained a group of Cuban refugees for an invasion of Cuba. Called the 2506 Brigade, it consisted of only about 1,300 men, most of them young and inexperienced volunteers. But their sponsors expected that their arrival would spark a large-scale rebellion in Cuba.

In January 1961, three months before the invasion was to take

place, John F. Kennedy became President of the United States. Informed of the planned invasion, Kennedy insisted that U.S. forces should not take any public part in it. The CIA chief assured him that would not be necessary.

On April 15, two days before the scheduled landing, Cuban-exile pilots began to bomb the invasion site at the Bay of Pigs. Alerted by the air attack, Castro sent his own forces to the area. When the 2506 Brigade landed, it faced tanks and heavy artillery fire. Kennedy refused requests for U.S. air support of the invasion.

Though the invading soldiers faced insurmountable odds, they fought bravely. But after four days, the invasion collapsed and the surviving 1,100 men were taken prisoner. After spending more than a year in Cuban jails, the prisoners were ransomed with $53 million worth of food and medicine.

Small groups of exiles began to plan for another invasion. But after the Cuban Missile Crisis of 1962 took the United States and the Soviet Union to the brink of nuclear war, Kennedy pledged that the United States would not try to overthrow Castro's government by force.

Although Cuban exiles continued to toast each other with sentiments like "Next year in Havana," it became increasingly apparent that Castro would not soon disappear. In 1978, some exiles began what came to be called *El Diálogo* (the dialogue)—an attempt to negotiate with Castro's government. They persuaded Castro to allow exiles to return for brief visits to family members in Cuba.

Even though 250,000 Cuban Americans traveled to Cuba during the next few years, hard-line exiles denounced those who had begun the dialogue. In the hardliners' view, there should be no cooperation—only steadfast opposition to the Castro regime.

The year 1980 was an important turning point for the Cuban American exiles. The Mariel boatlift, organized and operated by Cuban Americans, brought thousands of new immigrants into south Florida. Among them were many who were of African origin, from the poorer classes of Cuba, and less educated than the earlier immigrants. It was impossible to find housing for them all, and many lived in tents along the streets of Miami's Little Havana.

The Marielitos were a frightening sight to the Anglos of Dade County. Later that year, Anglo voters turned out in large numbers to vote to overturn Dade County's bilingual status. The election result was a shock to Miami's Cuban Americans, who felt that they had earned an equal place in the community.

Cuban exiles began to take an active role in politics, both locally and nationally. They began to take

out citizenship papers so that they could vote. In the 1980s, the term *exile* gave way to a new designation for themselves: Cuban Americans. It signified their acknowledgment that their stay here would not be temporary.

In 1981, a group of Cuban American business leaders organized the Cuban American National Foundation (CANF). From its headquarters in Washington, D.C., the CANF lobbied Congress to take stronger action against Castro's government. The lobbying effort was responsible for

Within the tightly knit Cuban American communities, people kept close ties with their friends and neighbors from Cuba. Family members and friends gather for this group shot in the 1950s.

the creation of a radio and a television station that beamed anticommunist programs into Cuba. The CANF's political arm, the Free Cuba Committee, collected funds to contribute to sympathetic political candidates.

Another organization, Facts About Cuban Exiles (FACE), was formed to counteract anti-Cuban stereotypes in the media and to promote a better image of Cuban

Americans. FACE soon had chapters in Cuban American communities throughout the country.

Dade County's Cuban Americans had long resented the editorial stance of the *Miami Herald*, the city's leading newspaper. The *Herald* seemed to speak only for the Anglo community, and posters in Little Havana declared, "Yo no creo en El *Herald*" (I don't believe in the *Herald*). In the 1980s, the newspaper's owners responded to the growing influence of the Cuban American community. They started a Spanish-language edition, *El Nuevo Herald*, and hired Cuban American journalists for the English-language paper as well. Ramón Mestre, who had earlier chained himself to the front door of the *Herald*'s offices to protest its coverage of the Cuban community, was now named to the paper's editorial board.

Political organization also led to victories by Cuban American candidates at the polls. In 1985, Xavier Suárez won the first of three terms as the mayor of Miami. In 1988, Dade County's voters elected Ileana Ros-Lehtinen as the first Cuban American to serve in Congress. Two others—Lincoln Diaz-Balart from Florida and Robert Menendez from New Jersey—have joined her there.

Inevitably, life in the United States has changed the Cuban exiles and their culture. The extended family was the strongest force in Cuban society. Its roots lie in Spanish culture, which was male-dominated. The father was the unquestioned head of the family; his wife served as a mediator between him and their children. Grandparents, uncles, and aunts on both sides were given the same respect as parents.

Thus, one of the most devastating effects of the mass emigration from Castro's Cuba was the splintering of families. Often, mothers and children left Cuba first. It was more difficult for adult males to leave because men between ages 14 and 45 were subject to the military draft.

Even when families were later reunited in the United States, conditions here changed them. In the struggle to survive, it became necessary for many wives to work. This lessened the authority of the husbands. There has, in fact, been a relatively high divorce rate among Cuban Americans.

Most of the early Castro-era immigrants insisted that their children continue to speak Spanish and tried to uphold traditional family values. But children born in the United States and those who arrived at a young age began to absorb the values of a different culture from U.S. schools and television programs.

Yet some older traditions have survived. Among the most popular is the *quinceañera,* the celebration of a young woman's 15th birthday. This occasion sometimes takes on lavish proportions. One father rented Miami's football stadium, the Orange Bowl, for the guests at his daughter's *quinceañera.*

Cuban Americans have tried to maintain a sense of community spirit by forming *municipios*—associations of people who came from the same district in Cuba. Members of the *municipios* elected town councils and mayors—just as if they were in Cuba—and provided, and still provide, help in finding homes and jobs for new arrivals from their districts. At *municipio* social gatherings, people meet others with similar memories of life in Cuba.

The Catholic Church provided important services in bringing Cu-

The wedding party of Noel and Deborah Morales poses for a formal portrait.

ban refugees to the United States and resettling them after their arrival. Castro expelled Catholic priests from the island in 1961, and many were reassigned to parishes in the Archdiocese of Miami. One of them, Agustín Román, is now an auxiliary bishop of Miami.

Most refugees have retained their Catholicism, along with the religious traditions that are unique to Cuba. Devotion to the patroness of Cuba, Nuestra Señora de la Caridad (Our Lady of Charity) has remained popular. Many Cuban American homes have outdoor shrines to her or to other favorite saints. On her feast day, September 8, Our Lady of Charity is honored with processions and special masses. January 6, the feast of Los Tres Reyes Magos (the Three Kings, or Magi) is another occasion when Cuban Americans celebrate their faith in public ceremonies. The Tres Reyes procession down Calle Ocho in Miami attracts hundreds of thousands of people.

The large number of Africans who were brought to Cuba preserved elements of their own religion. Over the years, it blended with Catholicism to produce a faith called Santería. African gods, called *orishas,* became identified with Catholic *santos,* or saints. Followers of Santería make offerings to the *santos*—sometimes by sacrificing an animal—to ask for favors. Santería houses of worship are found in most large Cuban American communities. Some of the beliefs of Santería are followed by Cubans of purely Spanish heritage.

Most Castro-era Cuban immigrants expected to return to their homeland. But for some, their sojourn in the United States has now extended into its fourth decade. The Cuban American community has grown to include a second and a third generation. The majority of Cuban Americans have never experienced life in Cuba—they are native-born citizens of the United States. Like members of other immigrant groups, they have put down roots and made their claim to part of the American dream.

In Cuba, blacks and whites (and people of all shades) could belong to the same clubs and associations. Florida, however, had a system of segregation that strictly separated the races. As a result, black Cubans in Florida formed their own clubs, like the Union Martí-Maceo. Shown here is a dinner of Coca-Cola employees at the club around 1940.

A sidewalk café at El Pasaje, a famous hotel and restaurant in Ybor City, Florida, during the 1920s.

COMMUNITIES

Gustavo Pérez Firmat, a literary critic and memoirist, described Miami's Little Havana in the 1960s.

During those early years of exile, Cuban Miami was a small, tightly knit community of families struggling hard to make ends meet. Since we knew we were better than our circumstances, there was no shame or embarrassment at being poor. For the grown-ups, the principal goal was to make do until the return to the beloved island. For the children, America was an adventure. Almost every week we went to the airport to meet relatives or friends arriving from Cuba. Those were the days when one could go up on the roof of the terminal and wave and call out to the people getting off the plane onto the tarmac. We were there the day my old teachers, the Christian Brothers from La Salle, arrived en masse. After greeting them at the airport, a throng of former students and their parents went to the hotel in Downtown Miami where the Brothers were going to stay. In the lobby of the hotel, surrounded by small groups of people, each of the Brothers held court in his black suit with the white ecclesiastical collar. I remember seeing Hermano Victoriano, the feared vice-principal, describing how the Catholic schools were shut down and the horrors of the Revolution. As always, the bad news was good news, for it filled us with hope and anticipation.

Oh, the good old exile days. It was exciting sleeping three or four to a room, having people come and go all the time, packing everybody into the Rambler and going to the Tropicaire drive-in on a steamy summer night. In spite of the language barrier, school in the States was easier than it had been at La Salle. And the classes were full of girls! (My Cuban school had been for boys only.) Falling in love with the *americanas*, which Rego and I did with clockwork regularity, was a thrill. Unlike many of the Cuban girls, they would actually let you hold their hand and kiss them.

Luis Botifill, who became a successful businessman and banker in Miami, described the problem of exile.

It will always be difficult for you Americans to understand the realities as we Cubans in Miami see them. Immigrants want to assimilate because, by and large, they have brought with them unhappy memories of their native countries. But we don't have bad memories of Cuba. Before 1959, we did not think the U.S. was better. We thought *Cuba* was better. And most of us still do. It isn't that I am not grateful to the United States, or that I don't love the United States. I

At this New York Cuban social center in the 1950s, portraits of Abraham Lincoln and George Washington appear on the wall along with Cuban heroes.

do. But even though this country has been very good to me, even after thirty-three years I don't feel comfortable here. And the reason is simple. I would rather be in Cuba.

Gisela Feil was born in Cuba in 1943 to parents who had immigrated to the island from Romania. She left Cuba and came to the United States with her mother in 1962. Her sister was already married and settled in Indiana. Gisela trained as a social worker and has lived in Indiana as well as Miami.

There's the mobility—moving from Chicago to Miami—but in Cuba you were in Havana, and you were in the same house for twenty years. I only moved two times in my whole life in Cuba, and now I move every two years. That in itself shows we were so dependent. I haven't been to Miami for over two years, but when I was there, I noticed that if one Cuban is doing something, at least a hundred more are doing the same thing. You know, like the Marielitos—everybody was getting their families from Cuba, or everybody was going to Cuba for a visit. How can I say—they repeat; they are very interdependent. You have to wear the same type of shoes or colors. Whatever it is, it's like, "Yes, do it." That's so scary, because politically, I think they influence each other a lot. Everybody has to vote for the same person, and that is a strong political thing. In Miami you feel like you left Cuba because you hated Castro, and you have to think like that. If you change your mind, they isolate you like the Amish do—outcasts. They'll say some nasty words to you. They feel they have to live through your life, and I don't know why. There is no respect for independence at all. That is one of the negative things about Miami I really don't appreciate at all....

I want to be close, but not that close. I love to go there, like I'm going this summer. It's nice for the moment, but it's nice to leave again because you live in such a pressure of what other people think of you.

I know many people who were dirt poor in Cuba, and who came here and did well, who have totally blocked the idea that they were ever needy in Cuba. I remember one woman who I know for a fact used to eke out a living taking in laundry in Havana—I know because in the old days my mom used to help her out when she could—and now that she's doing well here talks about herself in Cuba as if she had belonged to a family of sugar mill owners....

But I can't help feeling that if this woman could go back to Cuba, the way someone who comes from the Dominican Republic or Jamaica can go back, she would realize, "No, I made my way in the U.S. If I'd stayed in Cuba, I'd probably still be poor." But of course she can't go back and these kinds of myths acquire a life of their own.

—David Rosemond, an Afro-Cuban immigrant

As Others Saw Them

Two things happened in the next years that caused all money for development of tourism in South Florida to dry up. One, Disney World [in Orlando, 225 miles north of Miami] started operating, and everybody with big money in New York knew it, they knew that 80 percent of the tourists who came to Florida came by car and Disney World would be like a Chinese Wall—nobody would drive further into South Florida. The second factor was the jet plane. It became just as cheap to fly to Jamaica or Puerto Rico, where you can get two weeks of sunshine guaranteed, than to fly to Miami, where you may get two weeks of rain if you're unlucky.

Had it not been for the Cubans, Miami would have been a dead duck. We had an economic depression in 1959; 1960 was a total disaster. The United Way failed, it did not raise one-third of its goal.... The Cubans moved into a vacuum; the place was full of empty stores. Southwest Eighth Street was boarded up from one end to the other. Very soon they went into the export-import business, they went into banks and everything else; they became the liaison between the United States and Latin America.

—Monsignor Bryan D. Walsh, administrator of the Pedro Pan program, describing the economic situation in Miami in the 1960s

The second-largest Cuban American community, after Miami, is in Union City, New Jersey, just across the Hudson River from New York City. Manuel Alvarez, who came to the United States with his parents in 1962, when he was 14, now lives in Union City. He described the ties between his community and Miami.

People here always want to move to Miami or South Florida. But a lot of times they find they miss it here. Just about everyone who has moved to Miami has family here. People come back. I may be the only Cuban in Union City who doesn't have a lot of family in Miami....

Those that [originally] came to Miami only heard the propaganda [that Castro would soon be overthrown and they could return to Cuba]. Those that came to the North had a much more open perspective. I think the reality of feeling a different kind of weather and having to bundle up gives you more time to reflect and makes you realize that the world is more than Cuba.

Barry Moreno is a librarian at the Statue of Liberty/Ellis Island National Monument. He was born in Los Angeles in 1965 to parents who were Cuban immigrants. Moreno told an interviewer about the community in which he grew up.

We weren't really in a neighborhood that was Cuban, except for our relatives and some friends of my father's and mother's. We were in mostly Mexican American neighborhoods. We were very politicized when we were young, though. We were taught that Castro was evil and that anything had to be done to get him out of power. He was sort of an image of evil in our family. So therefore when I was quite young, everything was politics. I started reading newspapers every day and keeping an eye on political events. So it made me very interested in politics, especially Republican politics. We were all Republicans. I remember as a child, Governor Reagan was a hero to me. My first name, Barry, is from Barry Goldwater, who was defeated for president in 1964. He was a hero to many Cubans.

Many Cuban children in Key West went to the San Carlos Institute. Downstairs from the school was a movie theater and the office of the Cuban consul. These students in the 1940s review a parade in front of the school. In the center is the queen of the parade.

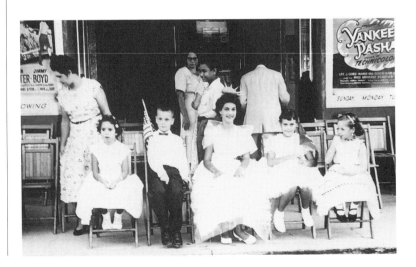

Carlos Garcia, who came to New York in 1946, recalled the gathering places where Cubans of that era met one another.

We always have contacts in restaurants and barbers' shops and places. Cubans went to this place called La Salle. La Salle was a cafeteria in Seventh Avenue and Fifty-first Street. Very famous. A lot of musicians went there, Cuban musicians including Desi Arnaz used to be there. I knew him very well. I have a hat that he gave me. And all the Cubans, musicians and show-business people, they were always here from Cuba. In fact, two blocks down, in the Brass Rail restaurant, Camilo Cienfuegos [who later became a high official in Castro's government] was a busboy there—the guy who cleans the tables and puts out the bread and butter. Camilo was twenty-eight, maybe thirty. Tall guy. Very, very happy guy, always laughing, very optimistic. Very optimistic, Camilo.

Adjusting to a new culture was part of the adventures that Hamlet Arias recalled for an interviewer. With his mother and grandmother, he lived in a Latino neighborhood in New York City in the 1980s.

We stayed with my aunt and uncle, who had already been here about 15 years. We lived in their apartment in Washington Heights for a month or two and then found an apartment close by. I went to school at P.S. and I.S. 187.

I was never awestruck by anything in New York, because I was so young. I had seen a city, a farm. Nothing was new to me except that the people were bigger.

My mother was awestruck when she first came. Have you seen the movie *Moscow on the Hudson*? When Robin Wil-

This public swimming pool is located in a New York City neighborhood where many Cubans and Puerto Ricans lived. The two groups often socialized and formed mutual-aid associations.

Employees and customers of Club Havana in New York City in the early 1950s. Here, Cuban Americans could listen to music and dance the mambo and cha-cha, which originated in Cuba.

Four men play dominoes at an outdoor table in Little Havana in the 1970s. Dominoes is as popular among Cuban Americans as checkers or chess.

A municipio *is an organization of people from the same community or city in Cuba. This group of* municipio *leaders met in Miami in the 1970s. Like many Cubans who had fled to the United States, they regarded themselves as exiles, not immigrants.*

liams was in a supermarket, and he went crazy over all the different kinds of coffee? That happened to my mother. Because she loves coffee.

What amazed me the most was my grandmother. She got around the city like she knew it. On the buses and the stores, made change in American money. She took me sightseeing around the city. And who is she? She had never been here before. She passed away, it will be a year next month. She really raised me. She brought me here, made sure that I had everything I wanted. She tried to spoil me, but I wouldn't let her. Because I could never stand the spoiled brats I knew at P.S. 187 who always had everything. They'd say, "Look at the new game I got." I'd be like, "Oh, yeah," and then I bought it the next day.

There were a lot of bullies. Something that always struck me when I was a kid was these TV programs about kids who were scared of bullies. And their father goes and talks to the other guy's father. I would say, "That never happened." I could never relate to American shows, because with the bullies I would always fight with them right away. As a matter of fact that was how I met my best friend.

I think that the hardest part for me, when I first came to the United States, was understanding the culture. I could never understand why people found things like Bugs Bunny funny. Watching TV shows, I would say, "Is that what these people watch?"

I didn't want to be Spanish, but I didn't want to be American, either. I didn't want to be anything. I just was very confused. Right now, I'm just somebody who's learning. A student of cultures. I still don't know what I am. I don't know my roots too well.

The writer José Yglesias grew up in Ybor City. In 1977, at the age of 57, he described his hometown.

The workers who settled the swampy area that Tampa officials turned over to the cigar manufacturers were not only Cuban. They were also Spanish and Sicilian. A typical Ybor City Tampan of my generation (I am 57) has, like me, a mother of Cuban parentage and a father from Galicia, uncles from Asturias and Cuba and at least one cousin or sister or brother married to a Sicilian. In Ybor City there is a Circulo Cubano and a Centro Español and a Centro Asturiano and Sociedad Italiana. They were wonderfully active cultural centers, for those cigarmakers knew how to organize more than trade unions, and two of them also built hospitals for their members, the best in Tampa at the time. All of them maintained a staff of doctors who served the members at no cost other than the monthly dues, and the American Medical Association bitterly fought these practices. The societies had to import most of their doctors, but there was one *americano* who fought the AMA ban, a marvelous surgeon named Dr. Winton whose first name, *que Dios me perdone*, I can't remember now.

These social clubs all had libraries, auditoriums, gyms, dance halls, and a canteen where the men gathered in the evening. At the Centro Asturiano we saw *zarzuelas* [Spanish operettas] performed by local amateurs. When great international performers, like Caruso, came to Tampa, it was the cigarmakers who booked them, not the *americanos* on the other side of Nebraska Avenue. Saturday nights young people (properly chaperoned) went from one dance to another at the four social clubs. I remember as a boy going to a free art class summer evenings at the Circulo Cubano. All the clubs were organized and run by the cigarmakers. All their officers and committees were democratically elected, and no one was paid for his troubles.

(There was a fifth club—the Martí-Maceo—and its formation is, perhaps, the worst example of the compromises Ybor City felt were necessary with the mores and laws of Florida. The members of this club were, in the main, black Cubans whom Jim Crow kept out of the others. They worked side by side with whites in the cigar factories and they were sometimes surreptitiously accepted as members of the Circulo Cubano, but they could not attend social functions at any or be hospitalized at the Español and Asturiano.)

A woman who gave her name as Magdalena left Cuba in 1969 when she was 12. After spending a year and a half in Spain, her family came to the United States in April 1971. They settled on the north side of Chicago. She described her community.

It all depends on where you're settled and what kinds of people you stay in touch with. I know that some kind of pressures, if you can call it that, is very real down South, especially in Miami, where there is a very large Cuban community and where Cubans are mostly in touch with other Cubans. Up North, it's different. For example, here in Chicago there is

Today the Cuban American community in Dade County has expanded far beyond Little Havana. Eloina Sanchez (left) and her daughter Olga Corrales Lino enjoy a chat over the fence of their house in Hialeah, a suburb of Miami.

Social service agencies offered help to Cubans, many of whom were penniless when they arrived in the United States. This couple waits at a clinic for a doctor to see their child. The sign on the wall reads: "Man loves liberty, even if he does not know that he loves it. He is driven by it and flees from wherever it does not exist."

not one particularly Cuban community. This neighborhood is kind of partially Cuban, but we are so mixed, even within this neighborhood, it's not easy to keep track of other folks. In fact, in this one building there is another Cuban family, and we know of other Cuban neighbors across the street. People don't really stay in touch enough. Like, just because you are here, you tend to pick up more of the American way of life and start breaking away from many of your customs, and that's the reality, at least for us.

When I was younger, I used to relate more to Cubans, partially because we could go out partying more. We had a lot of Cuban people our age, and we would go to dances, mostly Hispanic dances, and there you encountered a whole bunch of people, even the chaperones, because, you couldn't have a party without having all the chaperones.

Sandra Oldham, a physician in Miami, recalled why she chose to live there after first settling in Pittsburgh.

I came back to Miami ten years ago to be closer to Cubans. In Pittsburgh, there was almost no one who spoke Spanish and, in any case, I just never felt that Cubans were meant to live in snow. When they do, they somehow stop being Cubans in the same way. Here you have the same climate you had in Havana, and you have the coffee. Do you know Sarita at the Versailles? She makes the best cup of Cuban coffee in the city, which means, given the way things are on the island, probably the best cup in the world. You have the style, and the language.... In Miami, I can preserve and be close to many of the things that belonged to the Cuba that I knew when I was growing up. That's very important to me. I'm a roots person, you see.

People need roots, or at least I do. In Pittsburgh, the only Cubans I knew were myself and one other person. When I left, the Cuban population of Pittsburgh declined by fifty percent. And for me it wasn't a question of going somewhere like New York, or L.A., or even Philadelphia, where there are a lot of Spanish-speaking people; it was a question of my heritage, of my Cuban culture. I knew there were so many people here who shared the same past that I did. You know, I find myself in the ridiculous position of wanting to reassure you that some of my best friends are Americans, and that I love the United States. I *do* love it. But nobody outside Miami could possibly understand what it was like to grow up in Havana in those days, or to have been a member of the Vedado Tennis Club, or to have gone to the Phillips School.... Here there are people within a four-block radius of this house who can understand perfectly what it was like for me, whose own memories complement mine.

That's the point, you see. We all have these fractured, imperfect memories of what happened to us. It's not like that for you Americans. You can go back to your old grade school anytime you feel like it and say, "That's where I used to play basketball," or "That's where I kissed a girl for the first time," or whatever. But all this has been taken away from us, and what's more, if we did go back, we would probably find everything so changed that we wouldn't find the landmarks of our youth. But here in Miami, we have each other.

Dario Moreno, a professor at Florida International University, described the lure of Miami.

From the moment I arrived, I knew I had returned to the Cuba that my parents had always described to me when I was a kid growing up in Los Angeles. They always talked about Cuba with such love that anyone would have had to be completely heartless not to want to buy in. And Miami is the only place where the Cuba they loved and taught me to love still exists. The way things are going on the island, that may never change, which only makes me love Miami that much more. But mostly, I like being here for exactly the same reason you would have heard from a lot of other people here: As a Cuban, I just feel at home in Miami in a way that I don't anywhere else in the world that I've lived in.

Raul Martinez, who grew up in Huntington Beach in southern California, recalled the attraction of Miami.

It's two worlds, two planets. Over in L.A., Mexicans try to learn English. I know people don't give them credit for wanting to, but they try. Here in Miami, though, every Cuban makes a big point of speaking Spanish. The Federal Express guy who comes here, who probably speaks English himself, and, anyhow, knows he's delivering packages to an English-language bookstore, half the time will only talk to you in Spanish. "*Debes aprender,*" "You must learn," he said to Mitchell [the owner of the bookstore] the other day. No wonder the people here go crazy. The guy's a Cuban. If he were a Nicaraguan, or a Costa Rican, he would try. But for Cubans, it's almost like being outside, at work or wherever, is practically the same thing as being inside the house with your family. And it is like family living here. No matter where you go in Miami, everyone seems to know everyone else. I remember when I first went to high school and saw everyone kissing each other on the cheek the first day, I got completely freaked. I said to myself, "Hey, wait a second, are they all related or what?" And my family changed too. We hadn't talked about Cuba very much in California, even though my grandfather was a pretty well-known amateur boxer there and must have had a lot of memories. But I noticed that almost as soon as we all moved back to Florida, he started talking about Cuba more and more, as if once he got here he was really a whole lot happier living in the past.

At an outdoor party in Miami, this cook prepares a large pot of paella, a Spanish dish with rice, sausage, and many kinds of seafood.

Surrounded by two maids and her children, Maria Ruiz Martínez Ybor enjoys an afternoon on the patio of her home in Ybor City in 1907. She was the daughter-in-law of wealthy cigar manufacturer Vincente Martínez Ybor, founder of Ybor City.

FAMILY

Dr. Rosa Vazquez, born in Cuba, raised in Puerto Rico, and now a successful psychologist in New York, described the importance of family traditions in forming her identity.

I grew up eating rice and black beans. Not red beans like the Puerto Ricans and the Dominicans. Black beans. I grew up loving pork, which I think in the end was my father's worst enemy. But he loved it. My father was an excellent cook. He developed what he said was an exile palate. He learned it in Honduras because he had to cook for all the men which were together in this place who had fled Cuba. He was wonderful, fantastic, he could cook anything that you asked him. And he was the one who cooked the roasted pig Christmas Eve. You know that's a big tradition on Christmas Eve, when the whole family gets together to wait for Christmas Day. *Noche buena*, we call it, "good night." And on "good night" my father was the star because he would roast the pig the same way he used to eat it when he was a little kid. He would look for the same seasonings, the garlic. He would put it in the oven with his own hands and he would spend the whole day watching that thing being cooked. And every year he had another way of cooking the pig. Christmas was tied up with the family, and the food, and getting together, and the dancing.

When a young woman is 15, she has her *quinceañera*. I didn't have a *quinceañera*. I was given a choice. Did I want a *quinceañera*, make my social entry like a debutante? But I felt my rebelliousness beginning, and I said, "I don't want to be a debutante. I want to be an intellectual." And I didn't make my debut. My mother was devastated. Because she had made her debut in Cuba. She had that coming-out party, at 15. And all of my Cuban friends had their coming-out parties. Incredible parties, with 15 girls dressed the same way. A *quinceañera* is when you're 15, you have this party and you have 15 girls. I went to their parties, I did it for everybody else, but I didn't have it myself. I was always into books.

Novelist Cristina Garcia recalled the strictness of her Cuban American family in New York during the 1960s and 1970s.

For me, growing up Latina meant I had virtually no privacy.... My mother's main objectives in life, it seemed, were to read my diary, open whatever mail I received, rifle through my purse, and listen in on my phone calls. This did not happen to my American friends. My mother said it was her duty as a caring *madre cubana* [Cuban mother] to make sure I stayed pure in thought and deed and to protect me from bad influences, which meant anything from smart-mouthed friends to wearing bell-bottoms....

When I was growing up, too, sex was the greatest sin known to womankind.... Even hand-holding, kissing, dating, were the gravest of transgressions. That all this evil could be swept away by a wedding band seemed a paradox, but this was the party line in my home. Not surprisingly, my brother wasn't subject to such exhortations. On the contrary, he was expected to exercise his machismo.

Rodolfo de León came to Miami in 1962 with his mother and brother. His father followed the next year. The adjustment to the United States was hard for his father and Rodolfo felt that he never had the same relationship with him again.

We were visiting some friends in Tampa when we got word my father was coming from Cuba. We drove back the next day to Miami. I remember I was very anxious to see my father.... He came over on the *Máximo*, on a boat, a big boat. I'll explain. You know the Bay of Pigs thing? People that were captured, somehow they struck a deal with Cuba, where they were sent ships of medicine in exchange for troops, these people; prisoners, mercenaries. So that on the way back a lot of other people came, too. Most of them were well off. So my father left the car there. And he didn't know he was coming. He couldn't send us a telegram or anything. He'd been trying to come. And we had heard that he was feeling bad. He was doing all these weird things. He was praying. At home he would fall down on his knees.

It was very hard, first time I saw him. He looked very different, and I just didn't react the way I used to. And ever since then I haven't reacted the same way. Before we left Cuba, it was more like Daddy, Daddy—you know, father. It was more he represented something else before, and now he didn't. Something had been taken away. He didn't have the power he had before, the image that I had of him.

Rafaél Solano and his wife enjoy a meal with their daughter in their Key West home in 1908. The Solanos were prosperous enough to afford an icebox (behind Rafaél), which kept food cold with blocks of ice delivered by the local iceman.

This successful Cuban American family entertains friends in New York City in 1955.

Through hard work, Cuban refugees rapidly made their way up the economic ladder. Here, in 1966, the Salcines family of McAllen, Texas, poses in front of their new home with their brand-new Chevrolet Impala. The family had arrived only two years earlier, with almost no money.

A children's birthday party at the home of Gilberto and Hilda Lino (the two adults in front of the door) in the late 1950s in Miami.

Oscar Hijuelos, the Pulitzer Prize–winning novelist, spoke to an interviewer about his childhood.

My parents came from Oriente province in Cuba, my mother from Holguín and my father from a small town called Jiguani. I grew up as the child of immigrants—my parents came to the States in the early 1940s, during the war. I have an older brother and we grew up on the West Side of Manhattan in a fairly mixed population of mostly working class people, in the New York of the 1950s and 1960s....

Ethnicity was not a major issue in those days, at least not in my household. My parents always spoke Spanish with me, while I got into the habit of responding in English. It's a funny thing, to this day I still have to search for a certain word in Spanish, but can go to sleep and hear completely lucid and complicated conversations in Spanish in my dreams....

The reason I've always been fond of *I Love Lucy* is because my father liked it. His two favorite television shows were *I Love Lucy* and *The Honeymooners*. He'd laugh when Desi Arnaz would go off into his little raps in Spanish. There was nothing else on television like it. Today everybody talks about Desi Arnaz as a stereotype or cartoon, but when I used to watch that show I thought: this is a Cuban guy who has a job and he's always worried about getting ahead. That reminded me of the people who would come to our house and visit.

Magdalena Garcia was born in Cuba and lived there until she was 12. In 1969, her family was granted visas to leave. After spending more than a year in Spain, Magdalena and her family arrived in the United States in April 1971 and settled in Chicago.

My parents had so many problems adjusting themselves, they just weren't prepared to deal with teenagers. They were going through a whole bunch of different changes and adjustments. If you don't have your own life put together and you don't have your own viewpoints in order, you cannot really help another person to come through. And that's just the kind of thing I guess I went through.

In my case, it was mostly nonrelatives—older friends and folks at church—who gave me support, because there's a great tendency among Cubans to stop living in the year that they left Cuba. Every conversation at a family gathering goes back to politics and this and that, and it's hard for many of them to get over that and look at a new life and deal with the real issues. I see that particularly, not in my own family, but with my older relatives who now have children of their own, and I said, "My God, when are you going to learn that your children who were born in this country don't care what was happening in Cuba twenty years ago? They just don't care. They don't want to hear about it. They want to talk about other things, like Boy George and the Culture Club." It's just a big gap, and to me it's just very painful to see how immigration breaks up families.

Maria Luisa Salcines, born in 1959 in Guantánamo, Cuba, came to the United States in 1964 with her parents and brother. The family settled in McAllen, Texas. She remembered fondly the closeness of her family.

I am very close to my parents and my brother. And I think the bond between us developed those first few years in McAllen. We shared everything. It was just the four of us and we were always together....

No matter how bad things were my mother always celebrated our birthdays. I remember eating cake and cookies, and drinking cokes only on those special occasions. Eventually when things got better, Mother began to make her famous bocaditos (a small finger sandwich with cream cheese, tuna and pimiento).

Later on Mother added codito [elbow macaroni] salad to the menu, gaining her status as the codito queen. Any time there was a gathering at our house, Mother made her salad. Macaroni was inexpensive and it filled you up. The longer we were in the United States the better the salad got. At first it was a plain macaroni salad with a few olives and mayonnaise. When things got better she added half a chicken and when we could finally afford it, a whole chicken.

To this day I have celebrated all of my son's birthdays with lots of bocaditos and codito salad. It has become a tradition and a reminder of my special childhood. I hope my sons will pass the codito tradition to my grandchildren.

In 1992, a former refugee from Cuba enjoys holding his latest grandchild in Miami. Though most exiles at first thought they would soon return to Cuba, they gradually made satisfying new lives for themselves in the United States.

A family gathers for a baby's baptism. Catholicism remains a strong force in the lives of Cubans in the United States, and many family celebrations revolve around such religious occasions.

Gustavo Pérez Firmat came to the United States from Cuba as a young boy. A sociologist and writer, he described the experience of being part of the "one and a half generation."

Only those immigrants who arrived here between infancy and adulthood share both the atavism of their parents and the Americanness of their children. I see it in my own family. My parents, who are now in their early seventies, have no choice but to be Cuban. No matter how many years they have resided away from the island—and if they live long enough soon there will come a time when they will have lived longer in Miami than they did in Havana—they are as Cuban today as they were when they got off the ferry in October 1960. My children, who were born in this country of Cuban parents and in whom I have tried to inculcate some sort of *cubania*, are American through and through. They can be "saved" from their Americanness no more than my parents can be "saved" from their Cubanness. Although technically they belong to the so-called ABC generation (American-Born Cubans), they are Cubans in name only, in last name. A better acronym would be the reverse: CBA (Cuban-Bred Americans). Like other second-generation immigrants, they maintain a connection to their parents' homeland, but it is a bond forged by my experiences rather than their own. For my children Cuba is an enduring, perhaps an endearing, fiction. Cuba is for them as ethereal as the smoke and as persistent as the smell of their grandfather's cigars (which are not even Cuban but Dominican).

New immigrants had to blend the two cultures in their family life. Sofia Rodriguez settled in Bluffton, Indiana. She and her daughter, Alicia, spoke with an interviewer about how their family adjusted to midwestern life.

Alicia:

I think sometimes I had a little problem about customs here and the way they do things. I think my parents kept an open mind and they wanted us to really blend in and I know it was hard for them to adjust to some of the things and some of the ways of life here.

There were some things we couldn't do—for example, slumber parties. We were never allowed to go to slumber parties, and I can even hear it with her grandchildren: "You should not let them go to slumber parties." And even dating, I had to be in at eleven o'clock, even when I was in college and came home.

Sofia:

I will never forget the first day my daughter said, "Well, Mommy, I have a date," and I said, "A date?" and we were shaking. But on the other hand, we had to get used to the fact that they were living here and they were going to live their lives and we had to teach them to handle themselves. We were

Charlene Marin Gobaira appears at the center of this portrait taken at her quinceañera on June 18, 1995, in Metuchen, New Jersey.

scared to death, because we didn't have those customs in Cuba. We had chaperones and we were used to that system, so it was quite a shock for us. We had to make difficult decisions against our own principles. About those slumber parties, sometimes my daughters misunderstood. There is one thing that for us is vital: the feeling that at the end of the day of work, the family being together and going to bed together and turning off the lights and knowing that our girls were in the room. It was awful for us to think that they were in somebody else's house.

Alicia:
One thing that I am really grateful for is the family aspect of our culture, to have a close family, and that is the main thing that I want to pass down to my children of my own culture: family togetherness.

Sofia:
In Cuba we lived in the same city, and on Sundays our entire family managed to be together, to go out together, and the cousins always played together. We have tried to keep that closeness because it has been very unfortunate that now we are in many different countries. Right now my sister lives in Mexico, my brother in Venezuela, and I am here. But even so, the cousins communicate with each other and try to see each other, so that when we are gone, the kids will know each other and come together.

A 1942 textbook from the San Carlos Institute in Key West, Florida. Lessons were taught in Spanish because most of the students at the school were children of Cuban parents.

SCHOOL

Pablo Medina, today a poet and teacher, came to New York City as a boy in 1960. He remembered that four days later his father took him to a public school.

It was a long brick building that ran the length of the [city] block. Inauspicious, blank, with shades half-raised on the windows, it could have been a factory or a prison. Piled to the side of the entrance steps was a huge mound of snow packed with children like fruit on supermarket ice. J.H.S. 167 was a typical New York school, a microcosm of the city where all races mingled and fought and, on occasion, learned. The halls were crowded, the classes were crowded, even the bathroom during the recess was packed to capacity.

On that first day I was witness to a scene that was to totally alter my image of what school was. On my way from one class to the next, I saw a teacher—who, I later learned, was the prefect of discipline—dragging a girl away by the arm. The girl, trying to tug herself free, was screaming [curses at him]. He slapped her across the face several times. Most students, already practicing the indifference that is the keynote of survival in New York, barely turned their heads. I, however, stared, frozen by violence in a place previous experience had deluded me into thinking ought to be quiet and genteel and orderly. It was the loud ring of the bell directly overhead that woke me. I was late for English class.

When I entered the room, the teacher, a slightly pudgy lady with silver white hair, asked if I had a pass. I did not know what a pass was but I answered no anyway. It was my first day and I had gotten lost in the halls.

"Well, in that case, young man, you may come in."

She spoke with rounded vowels and smooth, slightly slurred r's rolling out of her mouth from deep in the throat. Years later I was to learn to identify this manner as an affectation of the educated.

"Next time, however, you must have a pass."

Not that it mattered if one was late to English class. Much of the time was spent doing reading or writing assignments while Mrs. Gall, whose appearance belied that she was close to retirement, did crossword puzzles. A few days later, in fact, something happened that endeared me to her for the rest of the term. Speaking to herself, not expecting any of the students to help her, she said, "A nine letter word for camel." Almost instantaneously, as if by magic, I responded, "Dromedary."

She looked up at me. "That's very good. You have a nice complexion. Where are you from?"

"Complexion?" I asked.

"Yes, skin."

San Carlos Institute in Key West was one of the few integrated schools in the southern United States when this photo was taken in 1912. Girls' and boys' classes were separated, however. Most of the teachers and students were of Cuban origin.

Skin? What does skin have to do with any of this? I had never thought of my skin, let alone considered it a mark of foreignness.

"Cuba."

"Ah, I was there once."

Then she went off on a monologue of beaches and nightlife and weather.

Gisela Feil came to the United States in 1962. Although she had been a top-notch student in Cuba, she faced difficulties in school in the United States.

The greatest problem that I had in school here was the testing system. It was different from the Cuban system. I couldn't understand and follow some tests—in particular, the true and false, multiple-choice tests. I always said, "I don't understand the questions. Those tricky words don't mean anything to me, and they keep me from knowing the right answer." So that was the big problem for me. The testing system was so different that I had to fight to get my teachers to understand.

One professor suggested that I take an IQ test. It was a blow to my ego. He said, "Why are you struggling so hard? You probably cannot make it intellectually." And I said, "What do you mean?" And he said, "Why don't you take an IQ test so you can find out what that is?" "Just to see how intelligent I am?" I asked him and he said, "Yes." So I said, "I'll take the test." That was kind of humiliating to me, for him to say I didn't have the intelligence, when I just couldn't understand his questions. He finally came back and said, "Yes, you have the ability to study," and I said, "It's you who don't let me go through it." So we had an interchange of ideas, and he finally started giving me some tests with essays so I could show him that I knew my subject. That was the system I was used to from Cuba.

On his first day in second grade in Miami, Rafael Rodriguez, one of thousands of Cuban children who came to the United States in the Mariel boatlift of 1980, tries to follow along with "The Star-Spangled Banner."

San Carlos Institute is still in operation today, educating a new generation of Cuban American students. This is a kindergarten graduation class in the 1960s.

Rafael Campo, a poet and doctor, described his school years in New Jersey.

I grew up in an affluent New Jersey suburb. I was the darkest note in the white harmony of classroom after antiseptic classroom—I worried I made discordant sounds when I smiled or played....

I was also continuously embarrassed by who I might be then, as if my classmates had invisible ears pressed to my family life, so that they might hear the Spanish blaring from the crack under my door. I remember the fluorescent lights in those eerie classrooms, laid together in the shallow, upside-down graves of the ceiling. I felt backward and exposed in their light, as they buzzed all the time their commentary on me, telling me not to sing aloud because it was America all around me. "Don't be proud or pompous. Don't be different. Don't be musical. Don't be a sissy. Don't speak Spanish." These strange lights seemed the condensation of the absence of a tropical landscape, a sort of eternal snow raining down, a cold light of winter.

As a sad child I learned voraciously, eating up knowledge to fend off the starvation of my spirit. I knew I was "different," so I learned my new language very well. I began telling unbelievable stories and writing poems early in life, and I wonder whether my impulse to write was at first rebellious, engendered by a desire to revise the world, according to my own internal reality. My cardboard report cards, like my bed and all windows and every classroom, were a series of squares which contained me. My parents rewarded me for all the As which were held, like me, in careful, tiny square boxes.

Maria Luisa Salcines came to the United States in 1964 with her father, mother, and brother. The family settled in McAllen, Texas. Today, a successful writer and columnist, she remembered the agonies of school.

I was in second grade and felt like a creature from another planet. It had been three years since my family and I had emigrated to the United States from Cuba. The older I got, the more out of place I felt.

My spelling and grammar were not improving and the English language and I were at war. I hated having to learn English.

It made me uneasy and it confused me.

Every day I would sit in class and wish the day would go by quickly so that I could go home.

After school I would rush into my mother's arms and into the comfort of my Spanish language.

My parents did everything they could to help me, but they finally decided to hire Mr. Bloom.

"What a name!" I thought the first day we met. Bloom, isn't that what flowers do in the spring?

Mr. Bloom was a retired teacher who tutored children for extra money.

He was a tall, heavily set man in his 60s with a sunny disposition and kind gray eyes.

From the start I made every attempt at disliking him. During my lesson I would yawn, look out the window or scribble on a piece of paper. I wanted him to understand that I was not interested in learning English.

At the end of every lesson Mr. Bloom would read me a story. I tried not to listen but eventually realized I could understand almost every single word he said. He always read funny stories that made me laugh, and before long I began to look forward to our afternoons.

As we became friends I began to trust him and, like a flower in a garden that blooms from the warmth of the sun, I let Mr. Bloom into my life.

Slowly, without realizing it, I began to absorb that dreaded English language....

One day, as a treat for bringing home a good report card, Mr. Bloom invited me to dinner.

I wish I could remember where we ate, but all I can remember is reading the menu and trying to decide what it was I wanted to eat.

After a delicious dinner the waiter brought the dessert cart. My mouth watered at the sight of a strawberry pie topped with whipped cream.

I will never forget that day, sitting with my new friend and savoring my strawberry pie.

That day I decided I liked to speak English, especially if it meant I could say, "Mr. Bloom, may I please have another piece of strawberry pie with whipped cream on top."

Carolina Hospital was inspired to write the following poem while picking up her daughter at a Miami school:

Alma Mater

Half past three at school,
in an oversized blue t-shirt,
navy polyester shorts,
she sees a crowd of mothers.

I see me,
six again, with tears,
searching, my mother with a
flowery wide skirt and flats,
waiting in a 67 Ford,
under the same black olive trees.

I return to her
now
running, smiling, waving.
For hers are not hollow hallways.

They hold the echoes.

The children here attend a private school in Miami. Although most of their parents came from Cuba, they are taught in English. Some older exiles, however, worry that young people who grow up without knowing Spanish will lose their cultural heritage.

RELIGION

Soldiers taken prisoner in the 1961 Bay of Pigs invasion were released from Cuban jails the next year. These men (in T-shirts), who have just returned to the United States, say a prayer of thanksgiving at St. Ignatius Loyola Church in Miami.

Carolina Hospital, a poet who moved to the Miami area after the Castro revolution, described what religion has meant in her life.

Almost every Catholic Cuban family owns a statue of the Virgin of Charity, the patron saint of the island. She stands dressed in blue and white watching over three fishermen out at sea. The fact that she appears to three humble fishermen, of different races, and rescues them during a storm at sea is a comforting reminder of the power of faith in the face of human vulnerability. Cubans in Miami built a chapel in Coconut Grove in the shape of the Virgin of Charity looking out to the bay. Often Cubans gather here for religious, as well as political, reasons....

My mother never worked professionally, but she worked all her life as a volunteer for civic and church organizations. I remember going with her often to some of these places. Two of her favorite institutions were the Centro Mater and the Youth Center. Both of these places, run by the Archdiocese, serve infants, the aged, and troubled youth in the Little Havana area. Seeing my mother give so much of her time to others, in spite of frequent complaints by my father, gave me a strong sense of social responsibility....

I also attended Catholic schools, both in Puerto Rico and Miami, through the 12th grade. My parents could think of no other alternative. Consequently, sisters formed a big part of my upbringing. They were a mystery to us. Some were strict, like Sister Francesca who made us sit upright with our hands grasped together on top of the desks, at all times, others were kind and comforting like Sister Helen. Sister Jude we heard left the convent. That was a topic of much conversation, as were the dark secrets behind the sisters' habits and the convent door. Then, we constantly complained about our schools and the nuns, but now I credit my Catholic schooling for providing me with a strong intellectual, spiritual and social formation.

After college, and a number of years distanced from the church, I returned to Miami, with a daughter. I placed her in Epiphany, the same Catholic school and church I had attended. My husband and I actually sold a three-bedroom, two-bath suburban home on a half an acre and bought a small two-bedroom condominium in order to belong to the parish. For eight years now, we have walked our daughter to school and church. Our renewed and more mature faith is a central part of our lives. We pray together at meals, read the Bible and attend mass several times a week. In difficult times, our faith has without a doubt provided strength and unity for our family.

Barry Moreno, born in the United States in 1965, recalled the importance of religion to his Cuban immigrant family.

Religion was taken very seriously by my family, because so many members were involved with religious life. So various saints were particularly honored. St. James was very popular. St. Peter and St. Thomas the apostle, and of course above all the Virgin Mary.

When the New Year would come in, instead of having a celebration, our family would kneel down and pray the rosary.... We went to special Masses for Our Lady of Cobré, who is honored in Cuba. The special Masses are always in Spanish. There are processions connected with the Virgin of Cobré. There is an image, a statue, of her that is held up high. There are all these flowers around. Made by the women. Hand-made or they're actually real flowers, and they're thrown into the church at Mass. That I remember.

The pope was always venerated. Cardinals. I remember recently when I was with my godparents, who live on Staten Island, we went to a priest's funeral and Cardinal O'Connor [head of the New York archdiocese] was present. So my godparents, who are from Cuba, had a chance to meet the Cardinal. All three of us knelt in traditional fashion to kiss his ring. My godfather said, "Oh, could you feel the power? *El poder del cardinal.* What holy power he had." Very religious. That was typical, the respect for the Church and for the hierarchy of the Catholic Church. Virtually complete obedience to the teachings of the church. No questions were allowed.

I remember when I was a child my oldest brother—we were teenagers—my oldest brother questioned some of the doctrine, because he was studying philosophy. And it caused some discord and shock. Because no one ever questioned the teachings of the church.

Soon after Dr. Rosa Vazquez's family emigrated to New York in 1961, they moved to Puerto Rico.

I have memories about doing my First Communion in Puerto Rico. That was one of the big things that happened. The First Communion is a big deal. The girls wore long white dresses. We had to not eat any breakfast, for hours. So what happened to me the day of my First Communion, and it happened to me every Communion after that—I would pass out! I passed out at my First Communion because I couldn't eat breakfast....

I remember all the mothers...making these First Communion dresses with practically no money. And the wonderful things they made, with practically no money. We didn't have a house. My friends lived with relatives. We didn't have a bedroom for ourselves. We hardly had any toys. But here were our parents putting out this massive effort to clothe us. My mother felt it was very important to keep the traditions.

Marisella Veiga González wears the traditional veil and white dress on the day of her First Communion in 1965. Her parents sent this card to friends and relatives to announce the happy occasion.

Recuerdo
de la
Primera Comunión
de la niña
Marisella Veiga
González
efectuada en la Iglesia
Saint Mark,
el día 8 de Mayo de 1965,
St. Paul, Minnesota, U. S.

TIES WITH THE HOMELAND

This sign, on a fence at the beach in Key West, is a constant reminder to many Cubans that their lost homeland is nearby.

Business executive Ramon Fernandez came to the United States in 1961 as a young boy. He feels comfortable in his new country but often thinks about his old one.

Sometimes I have dreams, and I see myself walking into my grandparents' house in Cuba and I see them sitting there. She's just sewing like she's always doing at night, and my grandfather's smoking a cigar and watching TV. It brings back a lot of memories. The States is home. I have no qualms about it, but I'm still attracted to that little island, no matter how small it is. It's home. It's your people. You feel, if it's ever possible again you'd like to reconstruct what was there. You want to be a part of it.

When the Bay of Pigs happened I was just a little boy, but I heard other people talking about it and I knew some guys that were there and were jailed. You become kind of angry about that, but there's nothing you can do about it. But you think "If only they'd given air support," then things would have turned out differently. I wouldn't be here talking to you now. I just hope another time it will happen, and I feel, myself, that if the time comes and they try to do something and they say to me, "Do you want to go?" I'd be very glad to go in there and try to recover it.

Cristina Garcia spoke to an interviewer about the links between the Cubans in the United States and those in Cuba.

I do think Cuba is unique in a couple of ways. The Cuban exile experience, first of all, is fairly recent. It's only thirty years old, or so. And, secondly, Cuba is very close to the United States and yet so inaccessible. Unlike other Latin American immigrants who can go back and visit relatives

Long before the Castro era, Cubans in the United States made generous contributions to help their compatriots in Cuba. Here, a woman wearing a sash in the colors of the Cuban flag collects money at a gathering of Cuban Americans in New York City in the 1950s.

in Mexico, Peru, Ecuador, or wherever it's not easy to go back to Cuba and many people didn't—couldn't—for many, many years. Also, Cubans, particularly the first wave, came for political reasons, because they had to leave, not because they were seeking better economic opportunities. This made for an incredibly fertile soil for nostalgia. And Cuba is so close. In Florida, you're breathing the same air and swimming in the same ocean. It's a unique situation. Yet, those of us who came when we were very small and didn't experience Cuba directly are still in the wake of it somehow. While we speak Spanish at home, English is really our first language and so we're in a unique position to tell the tale from a completely different perspective than our parents.

Cuban exiles yearned for news from and about Cuba, as Gustavo Pérez Firmat wrote in his book Next Year in Cuba.

Inside our house [in Miami], the radio was always tuned to one of the Cuban stations.... All we wanted was to hear about Cuba. Reports from the island were our life's blood. The radio on my father's night table was always set to Radio Reloj, a station that told the time every minute and in between summarized the news. As the announcer read the latest from Cuba, the seconds ticked away in the background. This went on without surcease hour after hour, day after day, month after month, year after year. Every morning my father woke to the sound of the Radio Reloj droning in his ear, and every night he went to sleep the same way. It was eerie. Ticking away, Radio Reloj was like a time bomb set to explode at any moment, except that it never did. The one piece of news we all craved was never broadcast.

And yet each day brought new signs of the Revolution's deterio-

A group of Cuban exiles in Miami stages an anti-Castro and anti-Soviet rally during the 1960s. Though Castro remained in power even after the Soviet Union dissolved in 1991, the fervor among Cuban Americans to free their homeland has not dimmed.

ration. There would be rumors of an uprising outside the capital.... These rumors swept across Little Havana like hurricane gusts. Someone would call our house with a news flash and my father would in turn call his friends and relatives. Even though most likely it was a *bola*, a false alarm, the rumor bounced around unchecked. For years *bolas* of all shapes and sizes filled the Miami air, launched not only by ordinary citizens but by radio stations and the numerous exile tabloids, or *periodiquitos*.... I doubt that there are any Cuban exiles who at one time or another have not received a call from a friend telling them, in an agitated voice, that Fidel is dead. And if you were the one who got the *bola* rolling, chances are that within the hour someone would phone *you* with the same rumor that you set in motion....

For years we lived like this, in booms and busts, having a ball with our *bolas* and grieving when they fell flat.... Perhaps if we had been less prone to wishful thinking, we would have paid more attention to the American here and now; but instead, here and now collapsed into nowhere, and we lived dreaming about the island across the water.

During the Presidency of Jimmy Carter, hostility between Cuba and the United States lessened. It became easier for Cuban exiles to travel to the island and make visits that reestablished family ties. The trips to Cuba were controversial among some Cubans who believed that they showed support for the hated Castro. Magdalena Garcia, who had left Cuba in 1969 when she was 12, was one of those who returned.

When we heard the talk about allowing Cuban exiles back, we got real excited about going back to see the family. So we did. Mom and I went in 1979. I remembered enough so that the whole scene wasn't new to me; we went back to the hometown, and I could go out and not feel lost. I remembered all my family, lots of neighbors and people. It was like going back to a different world. The people—even though they still know it's you, they look at you under a different light; you're a different person now. They couldn't help bombarding you with questions: "What's it really like out there?" Especially young people—their whole world is just so different. Even though girls back home are much more independent than my mom or my grandmother, I don't think they have been exposed to all the things that you're exposed to in the United States. The ideal for the girls, even if they've had a certain amount of education, is just to get married, stop working, and just raise kids or whatever. They just think differently. I would be a totally different person if I had stayed home.

Flora González Mandri came to the United States as part of the Pedro Pan program in 1962. Eighteen years later she returned to Cuba. She described her return to the family home in Camagüey.

Luz María [her aunt] had called almost everyone in the family to let them know I had arrived and soon the house was filled with the chatter for which I had been so nostalgic.... Each one took a turn at the microphone of the tape recorder I had brought to send greetings to those in Miami. They said that even though they never wrote, they always thought about them, one got lazy, you know, and besides, with all the problems we have, it's not worth writing about unpleasant things, but really, we often talk about you, and that comes from the heart....

When it was time to leave, saying good-bye to Luz María was very sad. I began to cry. I picked up my bag and put it on my shoulder. Raúl [her cousin] had a small motorcycle and was going to take me to the bus station on my way back to Havana. Seated behind him, I was moving much too fast, passing the streets of my childhood, recognizing Agramonte Plaza, where I had played so often as a child. Once on the bus, I began to cry and cry. People had warned me that if I started, I wouldn't be able to stop for a long time. Through the tears, I looked at the Cuban landscape. I had forgotten how flat Camagüey was. The sugar cane was of a delicate green on the horizon, and the palm trees stood up defiantly against a violet and rose-colored sky. The bus had a radio and I could listen to the music and talk shows. Instead of ads, the station had advice as to how to raise children, and even classes on history and semantics: one said poetess, not poet, when referring to a woman. The station break became very familiar to me: Radio Progreso, Free Broadcasting Station, Havana, Cuba, First Free Territory in America.

This Cuban exile rally in Miami in 1986 supports Nicaraguan rebels ("freedom fighters") who hoped to overthrow the communist regime in that country. Cuban Americans have often seen the struggle against communism as part of their own effort to overthrow Fidel Castro.

Jorge Mas Canosa

The hope of overthrowing the Castro government has been an obsession with Jorge Mas Canosa since he came to the United States in 1960. Although he is one of the most successful Cuban American businessmen, he is best known for his political work.

The son of a major in the Cuban army, Jorge Mas Canosa grew up in Santiago, a port on Cuba's east coast. As a teenager, he went to a junior college in North Carolina. While he was there, Castro took control of the Cuban government. Within a week, Mas Canosa, then 19 years old, returned to Cuba and entered law school. After he and other students organized anti-Castro protests, Mas Canosa had to flee to Miami.

In 1961, Mas Canosa joined other Cuban exiles in the 2506 Brigade for the invasion of Cuba at the Bay of Pigs. After the invasion's failure, he entered the U.S. Army. But when he realized that there would not be another invasion attempt, he returned to civilian life.

At first, Mas Canosa had to take menial jobs in Miami to support his family. In 1968, he borrowed money to buy Church & Tower, an ailing construction company, and he made a fortune sinking telephone poles for the local phone company. In 1994, his firm merged with a larger one to form MasTec, today the largest Hispanic-owned public company in the United States.

Despite his skill as a businessman, Mas Canosa was always most concerned with *la causa*—overthrowing Castro and bringing democracy to Cuba. In 1980, he started the Cuban American National Foundation (CANF) to lobby for a more aggressive anti-Castro policy. He planned a radio station to allow the exiles to beam their message to Cuba. In 1982, Congress passed the Radio Martí bill, providing public funds for the station. A few years later, the foundation opened TV Martí as well.

In 1992, the CANF lobbied Congress to pass the Cuban Democracy Act. It tightened the embargo on Cuba by restricting trade by subsidiaries of U.S. companies operating in foreign countries and it forbade ships that traded with Cuba from entering U.S. ports. Mas Canosa and his organization have become the most powerful influence on U.S. policy toward Cuba.

Lourdes Curro waves an American flag as she waits to be sworn in as a U.S. citizen in a mass ceremony with more than 10,000 other people.

CHAPTER SIX

PART OF THE UNITED STATES

L ucy, I'm home!" In the 1950s most Americans would recognize that refrain. Even today, a decade after his death, the most famous Cuban American is Desi Arnaz. The comedy show that he and his wife Lucille Ball created is still running every single night on some television stations. Its popularity remains undimmed, though it has been shown countless times since it first aired in 1952.

Significantly, Desi Arnaz in real life and Ricky Ricardo, his television persona, were both bandleaders. Before 1959, the best-known Cubans in the United States were musicians or athletes such as boxer Eligio "Kid Chocolate" Sardiñas and baseball player Orestes "Minnie" Miñoso.

Cuban Americans have had a great influence on the music of the United States. Mario Bauza, who first arrived in the United States from Havana in 1926, was a major figure in American jazz. Working with African American musicians such as Cab Calloway and John B. "Dizzy" Gillespie, Bauza developed the style called Latin jazz, CuBop, or Afro-Cuban jazz.

Combining African and European rhythms, techniques, and instruments, Cuban-born musicians introduced a series of dance-music styles to American audiences. In the 1920s, it was the rumba; during the 1930s and 1940s, it was mambo; in the 1950s, it was cha-cha-cha; in the 1960s, the boogaloo; and in the 1970s, salsa. Both Perez Prado, who popularized the mambo, and Celia Cruz, the "queen of salsa," attracted many fans in the United States. Gloria Estefan and her Miami Sound Machine are only the latest Cuban American musicians to attain popularity.

But it is just as significant, though less well known, that Desi Arnaz was also an astute businessman and judge of talent. He built an entertainment production company, Desilu, that created many other successful television shows and movies besides "I Love Lucy."

The Castro-era Cuban immigrants also displayed a remarkable talent for business. In the past four decades, the Cuban American presence has transformed Miami into what has been called "the capital of Caribbean America." The city has become a major banking and trade center, with economic ties to many South American and Caribbean nations. Indeed, Cubans have exerted a powerful influence on all aspects of life in Florida.

Today, prosperous Cuban Americans have moved beyond Calle Ocho and into the most fashionable suburbs of Dade County and south Florida. In recent years the region's population has swelled with Cuban émigrés who originally settled in other parts of the United States, as well as with new immigrants from Haiti and Nicaragua.

Culturally, Miami is today a Latin city as well. The Little Havana Arts Center, the Cuban Museum of Art and Culture, Florida International University, and Miami-Dade Community College are among the city's many institutions that sponsor the development of Latino art and literature. Several Cuban American journals publish the work of exile writers, many of whom continue to write in Spanish.

Like other immigrant groups, Cubans have carved out a niche for themselves in American society. They have added to the rich and diverse culture of the United States, renewing the dream of a nation made up of many nationalities.

Many accomplished Cuban artists—such as José Maria Mijares, Rafael Soriano, Osvaldo Gutiérrez, and Enrique Riverón—were among the refugees from Castro's regime, and have continued to produce their work here. Others who came here at a young age—Emilio Falero, Juan

González, María Brito-Avellana, and César Trasobares—started their artistic careers in the United States.

Cuban American novelists, playwrights, and poets have also earned acclaim and success. Some, like Caledonio González and Roberto Fernández, have written of the culture shock experienced by Cuban exiles in the United States. Cristina Garcia's brilliant novel *Dreaming in Cuban* relates the story of three generations of women in both Cuba and the United States. Afro-Cuban authors such as Reinaldo Arenas and Heberto Padilla have also joined the exile literary community in the United States.

Perhaps the best known Cuban American writer is Oscar Hijuelos, the son of pre-Castro Cuban immigrants to New York. His novel *The Mambo Kings Play Songs of Love* (1990) became the first novel by a Latino citizen of the United States to win the Pulitzer Prize for fiction.

Cuban Americans have contributed to their adopted country in countless other fields. Roberto Goizueta, head of the Coca-Cola Company; baseball player Tony Perez of the Cincinnati Reds; movie star Andy Garcia; Tania J.

A festival along Calle Ocho (Eighth Street), the heart of the Cuban American community in Miami. That city has a larger Cuban population than any city in Cuba except Havana.

León, the first musical director of the Dance Theater of Harlem; Modesto Madique, founder of a computer semiconductor company and later president of Florida International University; ballet dancer Ferdinand Bujones; singer Willy Chirino; Emmy-Award winning television writer Luis Santeiro;

and journalist Robert Suárez, now president of the *Miami Herald*, are among the many who have risen to the top of their professions.

Despite all this success, a shadow continues to haunt the Cuban American community— Fidel Castro. Since 1959, some Cuban émigrés have been waiting for Castro's downfall so they could return home. As Cuban American historian Lisandro Pérez noted, "Virtually everyone who came from Cuba in the early 1960s, as I did, had or knew of a grandmother who arrived here speaking only of going back to Cuba. The *abuelita* [grandmother] kept a packed suitcase in her closet so she could go back to Cuba once things were all right. She was not going to be buried in the sandy soil of Florida. The bag was eventually unpacked, and many *abuelitas* are, indeed, now resting in the sandy Florida soil."

Opposition to Castro remains a strong concern, particularly among those who still regard themselves

> "As a Cuban, I just feel at home in Miami in a way that I don't anywhere else in the world that I've lived in."

as exiles. Jorge Mas Canosa, the head of the Cuban American National Foundation, is the leading figure in the anti-Castro effort. Mas Canosa, who once worked as a dishwasher and a milkman in Miami to support his family, is now a million-aire. But his passion in life is to overthrow Castro and restore a demo-cratic govern-ment to Cuba. He has used his political influ-ence to keep the United States from establishing diplomatic relations with Castro's govern-ment and to maintain the trade embargo with Cuba. Some observers think that Mas Canosa will lead Cuban exiles back to the island when Castro goes.

How many would follow Mas Canosa? The majority of Cuban Americans have built satis-fying new lives in the United States. A survey conducted by Miami International University in 1990 showed that only 38 per-cent of Cuban Americans in Dade County would consider returning to Cuba.

Many of the "golden exiles" left property and wealth in Cuba, and some may still preserve the dream of reclaiming it. However, the more recent refugees—especially the Marielitos and the *balseros*—were fleeing a life of hopelessness and poverty. It is doubtful that they would give up the opportunities of the United States for a return to an uncertain future in Cuba.

In addition, a whole generation of Cuban Americans has grown to adulthood in the United States. Called ABCs (American-Born

A band performs Latin music for an enthusiastic crowd at a Calle Ocho festival. Before the Cubans arrived, Calle Ocho was in the middle of a Miami slum. As the main street of Little Havana, however, it became the center of a prosperous community.

Cubans), they have become as-similated into American life. It is doubtful that many of them would "return" to an island they know about only from their parents' stories. Indeed, that pre-Castro Cuba exists only in memory, for the changes in Cuban society since 1959 have been extensive.

Miami may be more like the remembered Cuba than Cuba is itself. Dario Moreno, a pro-fessor at Miami International University, told an interviewer: "From the mo-ment I arrived [in Miami], I knew I had returned to the Cuba that my parents had al-ways described to me when I was a kid growing up in Los Angeles.... And Miami is the only place where the Cuba they loved and taught me to love still exists. The way things are going on the island, that may never change, which only makes me love Miami that much more.... As a Cuban, I just feel at home in Mi-ami in a way that I don't anywhere else in the world that I've lived in."

Bilingualism—the use of both Spanish and English in government, schools, and businesses—has been a controversial topic in areas where Hispanic citizens are numerous. Many Cuban immigrants, like those in this damaged photograph from the 1960s, have attended adult English classes, after deciding that learning English can be an advantage.

Miami's leading newspaper, the Miami Herald, today publishes a Spanish-language edition, El Nuevo Herald. Miami's Cuban community regards that as a triumph, for when they first began to arrive, they felt that the newspaper opposed their influence on the city.

FROM EXILES TO IMMIGRANTS

Some Cubans have remained exiles. Amaury Almaguer is a prominent businessman and publisher in New Orleans. He came to the United States in 1980 after being released as a political prisoner.

I am 31 years old and ambitious. In the future I would like my business interests to grow and prosper. However, I did not come to the United States with the sole purpose of improving my economic status but, rather, to escape the political climate in Cuba. Therefore, if ideological conditions change in Cuba, I will not have a valid reason for remaining here. It will be difficult leaving this country, but at that time I will leave the United States with my family and begin a new venture in my homeland.

Marisella Veiga, a writer and professor at Miami-Dade Community College, came to the United States with her family when she was an infant. She described her sense of loss because she cannot remember Cuba.

Two relics from my Cuban wardrobe—well-made little dresses—hang in my closet. They are a way of getting closer to the once-possible me who was cut off. Larger attempts to understand were made. I lived in Puerto Rico and briefly, in the Dominican Republic. As a result, I have a sense of what it means to be an islander. Many of my adventures contain archetypical Spanish Caribbean characters. I can now sit with a group of "those who remember" in Miami and conjure whatever scene is called for. I know the cool privacy of a Spanish colonial home, what fried fish and plantains taste like at a sea-side stand, how old women hobble up to the cathedral....

A few years ago, I met a man who had left Cuba when he was three years old. Like me, he "can't remember." His family had gone to Puerto Rico, where he was raised. He had just finished medical school, and we were discussing trends in the profession. "But doctors today," he said, with some longing in his voice, "are not like they were in Cuba."

"How do you know? You don't know, do you?" I insisted. He admitted that he did not.

When I was an adolescent during the early 1970s in Miami, young Cubans (some of whom could not remember) categorized one another in two ways: there were *Cubanos* and *Cubanos arrepentidos* [repentant Cubans]. The latter described the more Americanized Cubans, ones who were "repentant" about their heritage. In the *Cubanos*' minds, the others who had adopted newer ways were ashamed of their heritage. It was in the '80s that Cubans, like other immigrant groups to America before us, began hyphenating their identities. Today, some describe themselves as Cuban-Americans.

Though not convinced it is an exact definition, I may begin to use the term.

In his book Next Year in Cuba, *Gustavo Pérez Firmat described his mixed emotions about someday returning.*

Much as I would like to think otherwise, deep down I fear that I belong with those for whom there is no going back: *no tengo regreso.* But my reasons are broadly personal rather than narrowly political. One does not need to be a political exile in order to realize that, quite often, there is no going back to the country or the culture of one's origin. For most immigrants and exiles, there also comes a moment when we must begin to define ourselves not by our place of birth, but by our destination. Paradoxically, for someone like myself, returning to Cuba would be tantamount to going into exile a *second* time. I'd have to quit my job, give up my American citizenship, completely reshape my life. I'm not sure that I could do it.

And yet the temptation of return remains strong. Even after all these years, the land of my birth beckons with the promise of a different and more complete life; and unlike countless other exiles and immigrants who have come to the United States, I may actually have the opportunity to bring this life about. As I write this, late in the summer of 1994, Cuba is in transition. The island's economy is a shambles, and public disaffection is growing. On August 5 thousands of Cubans took to the streets of Havana to voice their dissatisfaction with the Castro regime—the first time in more than thirty years that such a demonstration has occurred. Although no one can predict the exact timetable of events, it is certain that the Cuban Revolution has entered its final stages.

A mural on the side of a building in Little Havana depicts a blend of both Cuban and U.S. cultures. Alfred E. Newman, the cartoon character from Mad *magazine, strums a guitar and wears a T-shirt that proclaims, "I love Calle 8."*

Ileana Ros-Lehtinen

The change from exile to immigrant was made for Congresswoman Ileana Ros-Lehtinen by her parents. After the failure of the Bay of Pigs invasion in 1961, Ileana's father believed that it was unlikely that he would return to Cuba and took out citizenship papers for his family. His wife told a reporter, "He said you cannot educate two kids without a flag and a country. This is going to be their country and they have to love it."

Ileana Ros, called Lily by family and friends, was born in Havana in 1952. Fleeing the upheavals caused by the Castro revolution, she and her family came to the United States in 1960.

Exile stimulated Ileana's desire for success. She graduated from Miami-Dade Community College in 1972 and then earned her B.A. degree from Florida International University. She pursued a career in education while working toward advanced degrees. For 10 years she served as a principal of the Eastern Academy, a school that she founded in Florida.

Her father, who had worked for democracy in his homeland, encouraged Ileana to enter politics. In 1982, she ran for a seat in the Florida state legislature. Her victory made her a trailblazer, the first Cuban-born woman to serve as a representative and later as a state senator. During this time she met her future husband, Dexter Lehtinen, also a Florida legislator.

In 1989, the death of Claude Pepper opened up a seat in the U.S. Congress. Ros-Lehtinen announced her candidacy. Her opponent was Gerald F. Richman, an attorney, and the race was hotly contested. President George Bush campaigned for her in Miami. Ros-Lehtinen won the election, although the voters had divided along ethnic and racial lines. In her victory speech, she assured the voters that she wished to represent all the people of the district. She told the *New York Times,* "Now it's time for healing. I know there are a lot of people out there who feel alienated." She was the first Hispanic woman to serve in Congress.

Her achievements brought her an award from *Hispanic* magazine. She wrote, "Now, more than ever, we Hispanic women must re-energize and refocus our efforts to realize the vast potential that lies without our grasp."

For U.S. Cubans like myself, the change will be both liberating and perplexing—liberating because it will mark the end of a long historical nightmare, but perplexing because we will be forced to abandon structures of thought and feeling that have sustained us for over thirty years. Exile is disconcerting, but after three decades the possibility of return may be more disconcerting still. What happens to the exile who can go back but who decides not to? What does he become then, a post-exile? an ex-exile? After the demise of the Cuban Revolution, the question of what it means to be Cuban in America will become more rather than less urgent. I write out of the need to puzzle out what it means to be a Cuban man living in the United States in a time when I no longer will be able to think of myself as an exile. I write in the anticipation of the moment when I may well have to choose *not* to return to Cuba.

Maria Luisa Salcines, who came to the United States in 1964, is a writer and columnist for a Texas newspaper.

Most immigrants bring with them unhappy memories of their native lands. Cubans left their country because of political convictions. They have wonderful memories of Cuba before Castro. I am a better person for having to undergo exile. My family has prospered in this country and my husband and I can raise our sons in the greatest country on earth.

The end of communism in Cuba is near and when that day comes, many Cuban-Americans will return to rebuild the land they left behind. I will help my family in Cuba get back on their feet, but have no illusions about returning there to live. My life is in McAllen.

But there will always be a piece of my heart in Cuba. Cubans have a saying, "Next year in Havana." In my family, it's a little different. My father yearns to walk the streets of Havana. My husband wants to visit his grandfather's farm in Jovellanos where he spent his summers. My mother, brother and I want to return to our hometown of Guantánamo and visit my grandfather's ranch. My uncle still lives there with his family.

As Cuban exiles adopted the viewpoint that their stay in the United States would be permanent, they became citizens so they could register to vote. Heavily concentrated in Dade County, Florida, they became a force in politics. Pedro Reboredo told author Al Santoli how he became the mayor of West Miami.

I got involved in politics because my godchild's house was always flooded. In 1979, the South Florida Water Management raised our underground water table from one foot above sea level to three feet. This caused flooding after heavy rainfalls. Stagnant water would be in the streets for two weeks, like a lake.

I'm an engineer. With two or three friends, I measured the water levels in the canals that surround the city. It was obvious that a new drainage system would solve the problem. So I went to the City Council. I said, "Hey, guys, we have to do something about this problem." But the engineer who they hired said that the city had to spend $2 million to fix the system. I said, "No, that's too much money."

We debated back and forth on this for three or four months. I decided that the only way to convince these people was to get into government. So, in April 1982, I ran for City Council. And I was elected.

Salvador Longoria came to the United States in 1962 with his family when he was a boy of four. Today he is a successful lawyer in New Orleans.

Those Hispanics who lived during my parents' generation are to be praised for their many accomplishments. As immigrants, their main goals were to survive and educate their children. They socialized with members of their own nationality and tended to be divisive. My generation grew up exposed to different cultures. As a result, we emphasize similarities among Latin Americans rather than their differences, and we can interact with persons of many nationalities. Our goals include [raising] community consciousness and bringing forth a united community. I am happy that I have been able to serve the community, and I look forward to continuing this work in the future.

Novelist Cristina Garcia described her solution to the problem of Cuban American identity.

In years past, much of the immigrant push was toward assimilation: losing one's accent, making sure the children learned English so they wouldn't "get confused." The world has changed a very great deal in a very short time. Characteristics that used to be considered liabilities have evolved into tremendous advantages in our society and the American culture. I believe Latinos are increasingly becoming part of the mainstream, not by looking and acting more like "them" and less like "us" but by redefining what it means to be American in the twenty-first century. That definition is slowly broadening—and not because we're abandoning our multicultural identities.

Those of us who straddle two cultures are in a unique position to tell our stories, share our vision, imagination, history. Far more often, we're bilingual—and bicultural—than were previous generations. Our presence does not require anyone's blessing.

At last, I realize I do belong in two places. Two cultures coexist within me, if not always equally, then companionably. I can go public with my private, familial sense of Cubanness— and survive—while my Americanness also thrives. This doesn't diminish either of my identities but rather enhances both. I finally feel secure, comfortable, *whole*, with the hyphen between Cuban and American.

Most "ABCs"—American-born Cubans— have adopted the language, culture, and influences of the country their parents and grandparents regarded as a place of temporary exile.

PRESERVING THE HERITAGE

Desi Arnaz, shown here with a conga drum, was the first Cuban American to achieve nationwide fame as an entertainer in the United States. TV executives feared that his Spanish accent would not be understood by Americans, but the show that he starred in—"I Love Lucy"—became one of the most popular programs of all time.

Desi Arnaz described how he put his first orchestra together in 1938. Though he booked the group at a Miami club as a "Cuban band," none of the musicians was Cuban. One was Spanish, two were Italians, and two were Jewish. Arnaz demonstrated his ability as a showman by teaching his musicians how to play Cuban music, as he described in his autobiography.

The boys weren't bad musicians but we had no arrangements, they had never played Latin music, and...we needed a trumpet, bongos, maracas, conga drums. I had a conga drum with me....

And my mind did a flashback to the yearly carnivals in Santiago, when thousands of people in the streets form a conga line, and they go all over the town, singing and dancing for three days and nights to the beat of African conga drums. They also use frying pans, nailed to boards, bottom side up, which they beat with hard sticks, making a sharp *ding-ding-ding-ding it-ding it-ding-ding* sound, keeping tempo with the conga drum going *boom-boom-boom-BOOM*. It's a simple beat.

You can hear this sound approaching from ten blocks away and it keeps getting louder and louder and more exciting....

The conga had never been done in the United States. I went to the bartender and said, "Give me a bottle of Bacardí rum."

Then I went backstage to where the boys were....

That was the only time in my life I ever let a band drink while we were working.

"Listen carefully to what I play on this conga drum. It's four beats to the bar and the last beat à la Charleston, like this. And I hit *boom—boom—boom—BOOM*.

"Accentuate the last boom. The dance goes one—two—three—KICK. Now you...can do *boom—boom—boom—BOOM*, can't you?"

"*Sí, sí*, I can do that."...

By the time I got back from the kitchen with the frying pan nailed to a board and two spoons to beat it with, the rum was almost gone and they were ready to try anything....

I hung the conga drum's large leather strap around my right shoulder and started to beat *boom—boom—boom—BOOM*. The band started to join me.... The people in the club didn't know what the hell was going on....

I told them, "This is a dance, folks, called la conga. It's very simple...one...two...three...KICK. One...two...three...KICK."

And I played and danced to the beat.

Nick [a professional dancer] was on the dance floor and he hollered, "Follow me, folks, I know how to do that.... Get behind me. We'll form a conga line."

In a few minutes several couples got behind him. Then I jumped...to the top of the bar...and I did the dance and beat the drum from one end to the other and back again. From there I jumped onto the dance floor and pretty soon we had the whole...club doing this conga line.

And that was how it all began!

In 1995, Digna Olga-Blanco, who came to the United States in the early 1950s, recalled the Caribbean musical groups that played in New York City.

In New York you had all the beautiful Spanish clubs that I went to. They were beautiful places to go and see a show or go dancing. They were magnificent.

The place to go was the Hotel Taft. They had parties there almost every Saturday. The Baltimore Hotel, because they would rent rooms to people and there was a party. I also went to the Palladium, but I always liked Roseland best. We heard Tito Puente, Perez Prado, many many more. Puente was a cha-cha band, Prado was the mambo.

We all dressed so beautiful. I remember very clearly one dress that I loved was chiffon in hot pink. A full skirt with a very tight band around my waist and silk [bodice?] off the shoulder. Very simple, but I looked like a doll. I still have that picture.

Some nights, people wore maxi skirts. Other times, they wore them short, but not like now—just to the knee. And glass shoes, transparent, with rhinestone heels. Very beautiful. And white gloves.

Today, the young people have their own kind of music at

From the 1930s to the present, Cuban musical styles have spread to the United States. The Palladium, a music club in New York City, billed itself as the "home of the mambo" in the 1950s.

Gloria Estefan

The popular singer Gloria Estefan has fans throughout the world, but the Cuban community in Miami takes special pride in her achievements. For them she is "nuestra Gloria" (our Gloria). Her success represents the American dream.

Gloria Fajardo was born in Havana on September 1, 1957. Her mother was a schoolteacher and her father, José Fajardo, worked in the security force protecting Fulgencio Batista. When Castro overthrew Batista, the Fajardo family fled to the United States.

Gloria's father was captured during the Bay of Pigs invasion in 1961, and he spent a year and a half in a Cuban prison before returning to the United States. After serving in Vietnam, he suffered from a degenerative disease that would eventually take his life. Gloria, then a teenager, took care of him while her mother worked to support the family. It was a lonely and challenging time, and Gloria found that singing and playing the guitar helped.

In 1975, Gloria entered the University of Miami. While singing at a wedding, she attracted the attention of a bandleader named Emilio Estefan. She joined his group, the Miami Sound Machine. After graduating with a degree in psychology in 1978, she married Estefan.

By 1980, the Miami Sound Machine was her full-time job. Gloria improved as a performer, losing her shyness and becoming more dynamic in her act. She skillfully blended rock, pop, disco, and Latin music into the band's unique sound. In 1985, the group's album *Primitive Love* became a hit, selling 4 million copies worldwide. The Miami Sound Machine won the American Music Award as best new pop artist.

Tragedy struck, however, in 1990 while the group was on tour. Gloria's back was shattered in a bus accident in Pennsylvania. After surgeons implanted steel rods in her spinal column, she endured intensive physical therapy. Thousands of fans wrote letters to show their affection. The next year she had recovered enough to record a new album. In 1992, she gave a concert to raise money for the victims of Hurricane Andrew in southern Florida.

Gloria Estefan retains her strong ties with the Miami community. She told a *New York Daily News* reporter in June 1993, "I feel Cuban-American. Cuban heart and American head."

Roseland, but two days a week they still have music for the mature people. Sunday, it begins in the afternoon, and they play till about 10 or 12 at night. They have two orchestras, one in Spanish, one American.

Although Jose Vasquez is a successful businessman, he pursues a second career playing Cuban music.

In addition to my companies, I perform with the musical group Ritmo Caribeño and serve as their manager. When I was 15 years old, I played percussion instruments with a group called Jovenes de las Minas and enjoyed performing whenever we received engagements. My interest in music was rekindled in 1980 when a brother who is a musician came to New Orleans. We organized a four-piece band and played for personal gratification. But music is like honey and musicians are like bees, and gradually we added six musicians to the group. We made our initial professional engagement in 1986. Our repertory consists of dance music popular throughout Latin America, to attract our multinational community, and our popularity has grown by word-of-mouth. Recently we were nominated for the "Big Easy" awards presented annually by a local newspaper. We accept engagements for private functions as well as for large gatherings. Every year we play at the New Orleans Jazz and Heritage Festival and Carnaval Latino. Outdoor festivals provide a close bond between performers and the audience that is not found in other settings. For a period we played on weekends in a local nightclub, but when the establishment was sold the new owner preferred different entertainment. As a rule, nightclubs where Latin American music is performed are short-lived and consequently musicians wishing to work full-time in this field move to other cities where more job openings are available. Recently we recorded a demonstration record to send to nightclubs in other localities, to obtain additional work. Many bands from Latin American countries use this method to publicize their music, and it has proven lucrative for them.

I intend to continue working with Ritmo Caribeño in the future, using it as a source of personal enjoyment and added income. However, the majority of my time will be devoted to managing the three companies so I may provide my family with a steady flow of financial support.

Dr. Rosa Vazquez described the festivities that are sponsored by the municipio, *or association of people who came from her village in Cuba.*

I still go to my home-town festivities. In New Jersey there is a group of Cubans who come from my home town of Ranchuelo. We celebrate Ranchuelo Day. A big dinner. I don't even know half of these people. But they know I'm the daughter of Menéndez. This is actually on my birthday. I was born in the middle of my town's festivities. The patron saint of the town is St. Rosa, and my name is Rosa. So I was born in the middle of a party. My mother says that she was looking at the people dancing in the street, and her pains came.

The last one was held in New York in an Italian restaurant. We eat, and we dance. It's a big party to commemorate that day. I guess it started as a religious festivity. The Spanish brought their saints wherever they colonized. So every town had a saint, and every town had a church named after the saint. That's where everything happened in a little town. Baptisms, weddings, confirmations, communions. My town, the church is Santa Rosa. It's still there, and they celebrate that day in Miami, in New Jersey. I've been to the New Jersey party, I've been to the Miami party, with my parents. And I see people who knew me when I was born. Before I was born, they knew my parents. I've seen my parents' friends from when they were in grade school. These are big reunions. And they have a little newspaper where they publish pictures, and the names of people who have died, so you know what is happening. And they keep informed about who got married, who got kids, who

Mario Bauza, with his wife Lourdes at right, was a major influence on jazz musicians in the United States. Celia Cruz, at left, has won acclaim from music fans in both Cuba and the United States as the "queen of salsa."

BLACK BEANS

Black beans are a staple of Cuban cooking. They are prepared in many ways and accompany many other dishes. Black beans and white rice are called Moros y Cristianos, *or "Moors and Christians," in remembrance of the centuries when dark-skinned Muslims from North Africa ruled parts of Spain. The following recipe for black beans was adapted by Marifeli Pérez-Stable from a classic cookbook,* Cocina al Minuto, *by Nitza Villapol.*

INGREDIENTS

1 pound black beans [dried]
1 large green pepper, sliced
10 cups water
2/3 cup olive oil
1 large onion
1 large green pepper
4 garlic cloves
4 teaspoons salt
1/2 teaspoon black pepper
1/4 teaspoon oregano
1 laurel leaf [bay leaf]
2 tablespoons vinegar
2 tablespoons cooking wine
2 tablespoons olive oil

Rinse the beans and place them together with the sliced green pepper in a large pot. Add the water, cover, and let the beans stand for about eight hours. With the lid on, cook the beans over high heat for 45 minutes.

Meanwhile, press the garlic cloves, and cut the onion and the second green pepper into small pieces. Heat the 2/3 cup of olive oil in a large frying pan, and sauté the garlic, onion, and pepper. Add this mixture, the salt, pepper, oregano, and laurel leaf to the beans after the 45 minutes have passed. Cover and cook over medium heat for one hour. Then add vinegar and cooking wine, reduce heat to low, and cook for an additional hour. Add the two tablespoons of olive oil at the end. Serves eight.

became a grandfather, who had a success in their career. Like when I got my Ph.D., my parents wrote and told the newspaper about it. When I got married, they told everybody about it. It's keeping that tradition going. It's keeping the identity alive. This is who you are, and this is where you come from. And these are your townspeople. You don't have to feel lonely. You always have your family from your home town.

Irma de Leon, a judge in Cuba, fled the Castro regime in 1962. She talked about the importance of the Cuban heritage.

I always said I remember Cuba a lot, but I remember the Cuba before Castro. The Cuba when I was raised was different. I had all my family. The Cuba that used to be happy, but not this. But here, even though I am in the United States, I try to keep part of my culture, of my tradition. My husband always said that when the children were young, they should learn Spanish at home because they would have to learn English anyway at school. Even my grandchildren speak both languages. My daughter always said, "When the children come to your home, speak to them about Cuba, tell them about Cuba, because I want them to know they are part Cuban and part American, that we are proud and have a lot of things to be proud of." I am proud of my tradition, my culture.

Unfortunately, there are a lot of Cuban people that have forgotten, and they pretend that they are not Cuban and they don't even speak with their children in Spanish. I am a fanatic about history, and when I study history I learn about all those who sacrificed their lives to make possible the independence of Cuba. They gave everything that they had, and I am proud of that.

Here in Lakeland, we are a small community, but we always want to celebrate the anniversaries of our independence. I have been the one that started doing that thing. They always count on me to have special programs, like on January 28, the birthday of José Martí, our hero, who is like George Washing-

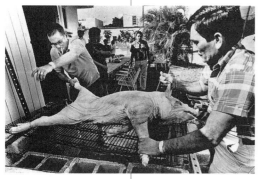

ton for Americans. I am very devout of his memory and I want to continue to celebrate that day because this is our identity; if we lose that, we will lose everything. Although I love this country and I am an American now, an American citizen, I want to keep this tradition. I learned to love this country before I came here, when I was in Cuba. But my country is my country. I have grandchildren that are American, since my daughter is married to an American boy, and I am real happy here in the United States. This is my second country.

Carolina Hospital, born in Havana in 1957, has lived in the United States since 1961. An author of poetry and fiction, she wrote the following.

I found myself, with my four-year-old daughter at my side, standing under a grueling 95-degree Miami sun. As we crossed traffic on Southwest 1st Street, in the midst of Little Havana, I caught sight of a street vendor from the corner of my eye. We headed in his direction. My hand shook slightly as I handed him the dollar bill. For Nicole, it was just a pink juice he was giving her. For me, it was her first *granizado*, my favorite drink as I grew up in the streets of Havana and San Juan.

When my family moved to Miami after my 9th birthday, I stopped drinking *granizado*, or, for that matter, hearing Spanish at every street corner. Many enjoyable pastimes were relegated to faint memories which occasionally surfaced because of comments at home. For me, they were just that, recollections. For now I stood with my daughter, on a crowded Miami sidewalk, reliving my past through this unknowing child. I watched her trying to gulp down the juice when her voice brought me back.

She spoke to me in English. "Mami, what do you call this?" "Granizado," I answered. "Gra-ni-za-do," she repeated with great care. "I like granizado, mom." At that moment, I realized that she wasn't reliving a past for me, but rather creating a future for herself, a future where two cultures coalesce.

The Feast of the Three Kings, on January 6, marks the end of the Christmas season and is a time of celebration. The Three Kings parade has become a tradition in Miami.

Andy Garcia

The Bay of Pigs invasion changed actor Andy Garcia's life. He recalled: "I remember hearing gunfire in Havana, and strafing from the air. Then I was told: 'We're going to Miami on Monday.' As far as I was concerned, it was just a trip. I was five years old."

Andy arrived with his mother, brother, and sister through Miami's Cuban Refugee Center. A short time later, his father joined them. The Garcias had to rebuild their lives. Andy's father had been a landowner-farmer and lawyer in Cuba. Now, he started a food catering business, while his wife worked as a secretary. Later, he sold the catering business and began to sell hosiery.

Andy was expected to help any way he could. He told a journalist, "After school, I used to go to basketball practice and then take the forty-five minute bus ride from Miami Beach to downtown Miami. I'd go to his warehouse and sweep the floors, get in the car and go home. And he expected that of me."

While attending Florida International University, Andy Garcia auditioned for a play. As he recalled, "That was when my true calling came out. And it came out in such force because I wasn't distracting myself with another activity.... I was lucky to have a passion for something."

In 1978, he headed for Hollywood. It was a long climb to the top. An agent advised him to get a make-over—fix his teeth and hair and lose the Spanish accent. He refused and was offered only small bit parts. It was not until 1985 that Garcia got his first big break, playing a detective in *The Mean Season.* Reviewers noticed him. Then he hit it big as a detective in *The Untouchables.* Starring roles followed—in *Black Rain, Internal Affairs,* and *The Godfather, Part III.*

Andy Garcia is proud of his culture. A fan of Cuban music, he has made a feature-length documentary concert film about Israel Lopez "Cachao," one of the co-creators of the mambo. He told a reporter, "Over the years, I've realized how much my feelings about Cuba define my sense of self. If the government [in Cuba] were to change, I'd want to go back to help the country."

Frank de Varona in front of his ancestors' castle in Villanañe, Spain. The castle is now occupied by the family of Rodrigo de Varona, a distant cousin. The first de Varona to go to Cuba arrived in the 17th century.

The baptism of Haydee de Varona in Sagua la Grande, Cuba. At left is her mother, Haydee Prado, and her father, Agustín Prado.

THE DE VARONA FAMILY

Frank de Varona has had a long and distinguished career as a social studies teacher and administrator in the Dade County public schools. He has written many textbooks and histories about the Hispanic American heritage. Among his many awards was one from King Juan Carlos of Spain in 1994 in recognition of his services to education. His wife, Haydee, works as a consulting psychologist for the Dade County schools and also has a private practice. We begin our interview with Frank de Varona.

Q: When did members of your family first come to Cuba?

One of my ancestors came to Cuba in the first group of Spaniards in 1511. Later, he joined the Hernando de Soto expedition that left Cuba to explore Florida in 1539. The first de Varona arrived in Cuba in the 17th century. I have visited Spain, where a member of the de Varona family still lives in the castle in the province of Álava that was built in the 12th century. During the Middle Ages, a woman of the family put on armor and went into battle—like Joan of Arc. So the king of Castile told her, "From now on your family will be known as de Varona." *Varón* means "man," and when the *a* is added, it becomes feminine.

Q: Could you tell us about your childhood in Cuba?

I was born in 1943 in the city of Camagüey. My father was a cattleman who had a 3,500-acre ranch. It was a wonderful childhood, and I had a loving family. In the 1950s, there were a lot of protest demonstrations in Cuba against the Batista government. I had an older brother, and because my father didn't want us to become involved in the demonstrations, he sent my brother and me to boarding school in the United States. When I was 14, I enrolled in Admiral Farragut Academy in St. Petersburg, Florida.

There were no bilingual classes, and I was put into the regular classes, where my lack of English was a handicap. We had to read *Macbeth* and *A Tale of Two Cities*, which even the English-speaking boys had trouble with. I remember when I sat down in study hall to read the science textbook. I began to underline the words I didn't know, so that I could look them up. I had been an A student in Cuba, and I was very frustrated.

Fortunately, someone at the school put me into the advanced Spanish class. We translated back and forth from English to Spanish. I understood all the Spanish, and was able to use the textbook to learn the English words. So my English rapidly became more fluent.

My great-aunt, my grandfather's sister Mercedes Cubría, helped me a great deal. She was a U.S. citizen and had been in the WACs in the U.S. Army in World War II and the Korean War. She was retired and lived in Tampa. She translated *A Tale of Two Cities* for me, writing it out in longhand.

I graduated in 1960. My parents and younger sister fled Cuba and came to the United States. My older brother was already here, attending Georgia Tech.

Haydee (standing) and her sister Carmen Manes in Cuba, where they spent their childhood. When Haydee was nine, her family fled the island.

Haydee:

I was born in Sagua la Grande, in Las Villas Province. My father, Agustín Prado, was a businessman. When I was four my family moved to the capital, Havana. I went to the first grade in Ursilinas Academy, a Catholic school. Then Castro came to power, and the school closed. My younger sister and I were taught at home by my parents. When I was nine my family decided to leave Cuba. I had an uncle who was in prison, and I remember my family taking food to him.

When my parents left Cuba, with my sister, my grandmother, and me, we went to Mexico. After about six months, we went to Guatemala, where relatives had offered my father a job. I remember my parents struggling a lot. My father was very hard-working and my mother very dedicated. They put me in a school run by the Maryknoll sisters. There I started to learn English. In my senior year in high school, my family relocated to Tampa, Florida.

In Tampa I went to the University of South Florida, but I wanted a more Hispanic environment so I came to Miami. As it turned out, my whole family moved there at the same time. Miami's large Cuban community made it a better situation for all of us. Eventually I got a scholarship to the University of Miami, and got my bachelor's degree in Spanish and psychology. I started working and also continued my studies in psychology at Nova University. In 1983 I received my doctorate.

Frank de Varona and a friend, Ana Maria Lamar, wear Mexican costumes for a musical play at a Marist Brothers school in Camagüey, Cuba.

Q: Frank, can you tell us the story of how you went to fight at the Bay of Pigs?

Well, I followed my older brother to Georgia Tech, planning to become an engineer. My father had managed to put away some money in a U.S. bank, and used that to pay our tuition. In March, 1961, the winter quarter at Georgia Tech ended and my brother and I decided to enroll in the CIA-sponsored military force that was training in Guatemala to invade Cuba. A relative of ours, Manuel Antonio de Varona, had been prime minister of Cuba in an anti-Batista government. He was part of the Cuban Revolutionary Council in Miami that was helping to organize the invasion.

Because I was only 17, I had to get written permission from my father, and he refused. He felt that it was all right for my brother to go, but what if we were both killed? My parents would have no sons. Finally, I persuaded him to sign and I arrived in Guatemala on April 1, 1961. After I had only 13 days of training, we departed for Cuba.

At a science museum with his classmates from the Marist school, 10-year-old Frank (far right) points to the giant turtle on display.

Frank de Varona (center) with President Jimmy Carter (right), U.S. Congressman Claude Pepper (partially hidden), and Dr. Harold Lannon in 1980. As principal of the Miami Edison Senior High School, de Varona had invited President Carter to visit.

Frank and Haydee at their wedding in 1991, with Frank's mother, Norma Sosa, who signs the marriage certificate as a witness.

I was very ill on the ship the whole time. I had gotten food poisoning in Guatemala, and hadn't eaten for five days. Because the ship I was on carried barrels of gasoline, no one was allowed to smoke or cook on board. I couldn't eat the cold canned food, so I didn't eat on the ship either. For three days.

As our ship was offshore, Castro's planes started attacking. One of the other ships blew up like an atomic bomb. Ours was hit too, but the captain ran it aground and we all began jumping overboard. I was carrying a rifle and wearing my battle gear—a backpack, grenades, and three bandoliers of ammunition. With all that weight, I sank right to the bottom. I remember looking up and seeing the light way above me. I ran out of air and almost drowned. But I managed to get most of my clothes off and swam to shore. I can still hear the cries of men who were wounded or drowning in the water.

After I was captured, I was questioned along with some other prisoners. Che Guevara [the Argentine revolutionary who was one of Castro's closest aides] came into the room. He looked at me and said, "How many caballerías did your father have?" A caballería is about 33 acres. I told him how many my father had, and he said, "Oh, so you came to take back the land."

I said, "No. If we were successful, my father would get back his land since he didn't steal it from anyone. He worked very hard for it. But I came because the Cuban Constitution of 1940 states that if a government abolished and trampled on the Constitution, the people have a right to rebel. So I am here because I want to restore the Constitution."

I told Guevara that the soldiers who captured us had taken away our rosaries and religious medals. Che Guevara made them give them back. I still have mine today.

Q: Then you spent nearly two years in prison.

We were sentenced to 30 years in jail, and sent to the prison on the Isle of Pines. We heard that Castro was asking for a ransom to let us go. The total was $62.5 million. When I heard that, I thought I would never get out.

People suffered terribly there. I was in a room made to hold about 20 people. There were 214 of us in that room, in nothing but our underwear. When we slept, there was not an inch of room on the floor. When we got dysentery from the bad food, there was no toilet paper, and everybody had to use the one toilet at the same time. Sometimes the guards searched our cells, made everyone strip naked and hit us. I have never gotten over it, not to this day.

Q: On December 25, 1962, however, you were released.

Yes. The Kennedy administration negotiated a deal with Castro. We heard about it when the guards told us, "You're going to Havana tomorrow and then to Miami."

My parents were waiting to meet us when we arrived in the United States, and they were overjoyed. But I couldn't feel anything, any emotion, then or for a long time afterward. The experience in that prison deadened my feelings.

I enrolled in the University of Florida to study economics and political science. After I got my degree, I joined the National Teacher Corps program of the Johnson administration and taught social studies to African Americans in the inner city of Miami and Dade County.

That was my introduction to teaching, which I had not planned as a career. But since then, I have remained in education. I was a principal, then an area superintendent and associate superintendent of the Bureau of Education. Today, I am Region Superintendent of Dade County's Region 1, which has 48 schools and over 60,000 students.

Q: If Castro were to die, or be overthrown, would you consider going back to Cuba?

Yes, I think so. After my retirement. But I have no idea what conditions there would be like. Castro has changed the society in many ways, not just economically. Cuba has many problems with crime, health, and environmental degradation, for example.

Q: We want to ask Haydee about her career. Have you taught, or practiced as a psychologist?

I was always interested in psychology. I work for the school system and have done assessment and assignments for special programs. I also have a private practice where I do therapy with both adults and children. I haven't taught in about seven years. I leave that to Frank.

Q: People have noted how successful the Cubans have been in the United States—as both of you have been. What do you think is the reason?

Frank:

Well, I guess it was the values we learned from our parents, which I have tried to pass on to my daughter, Irene. They believed in hard work and education. They sacrificed to send their children to college, and gave us the idea that we should make something of ourselves.

Haydee:

I also feel that they emphasized the closeness of the family. All the time that we have, we spend with family members. We devote a lot of time to them. Cubans have extended families, with close ties to grandparents, cousins, brothers, and sisters. The support family members give each other produces a sense of self-confidence.

Frank de Varona speaks at a reception to celebrate the 1987 publication of his first book, Hispanic Contributions to American History: 1492 to the Present.

Every summer, Frank de Varona takes a group of students to Spain. In 1994, with six of his students from Miami-Dade Community College, he visited Salamanca, Madrid, and other Spanish cities.

CUBAN AMERICAN TIMELINE

1492
Christopher Columbus lands in Cuba.

1511
Diego Velázquez de Cuéllar conquers Cuba. Within 50 years, nearly all the original inhabitants are dead.

1539
Hernando de Soto leaves Havana to explore Florida.

1565
In Florida, St. Augustine is founded; today it is the oldest city in the United States.

1819
Spain sells Florida to the United States for $5 million.

1823
Felix Varela, the first Cuban political refugee in the United States, goes to New York City. The decade sees the first Cuban immigrants arrive in the United States.

1868–78
During the Ten Years' War between Cuba and Spain, thousands of Cubans flee to the United States.

1870s
Cuban communities are established in New York, Philadelphia, Boston, New Orleans, and Key West.

1886
Ybor City, Florida, is founded; Cuban cigar workers begin to move in.

1895
Cuban exiles invade the island and start the Cuban War for Independence.

1898
Spanish-American War. The United States defeats Spain in less than four months.

1900
The Platt Amendment gives the United States the right to intervene in Cuba to protect its independence. The United States later used this clause to land troops in times of disorder.

1902
Cubans celebrate their independence.

1934
The United States abrogates the Platt Amendment.

1956
Fidel Castro and a small band of Cuban exiles land on the island, attempting to overthrow the regime of Fulgencio Batista.

1959
Batista leaves Cuba on January 1. Castro takes control of the government.

1959–62
The "golden exiles"—members of Cuba's landowning and professional classes—leave for the United States.

1960
The United States breaks diplomatic ties with Cuba.

April 1961
The Bay of Pigs invasion.

October 1962
The Cuban Missile Crisis brings the United States and the Soviet Union to the brink of nuclear war. The crisis ends when Soviet missiles are removed from Cuba and the United States pledges not to invade the island.

1962–65
Commercial air flights between the United States and Cuba are suspended. Cuban refugees arrive in the United States through third countries.

September 1965
Castro allows Cubans with relatives in the United States to leave through the port of Camarioca. Refugees in Florida send boats to help them escape.

1965–73
Air flights between the United States and Cuba resume in December 1965. In the following eight years, "freedom flights" bring more than 300,000 Cubans to the United States.

1966
The U.S. Congress passes the Cuban Refugee Act, which gives any Cuban who has resided in the United States for a year the right to become a permanent resident.

1973
The Cuban government discontinues direct flights between Cuba and the United States.

1978
Castro announces that he will allow Cubans living in the United States to return to the island for one-week visits to their families.

1980
Castro allows boats from the United States to pick up Cuban refugees at the port of Mariel. The Mariel boatlift brings around 125,000 Cubans to the United States.

1981
Formation of the Cuban American National Foundation, which lobbies Congress to take stronger actions against the Castro government.

1985
Xavier Suárez wins the first of three terms as mayor of Miami.

1990
Oscar Hijuelos becomes the first Latino citizen of the United States to win the Pulitzer Prize for fiction for *The Mambo Kings Play Songs of Love*.

1991
The Soviet Union is dismantled, and aid to Cuba is cut off.

1994
Castro declares that the Cuban government will no longer try to prevent Cubans from leaving the island by sea. Thousands of *balseros*, or rafters, leave. President Bill Clinton orders U.S. ships to take Cubans to the naval base at Guantánamo Bay rather than the United States.

1995
Clinton agrees to let the Cuban refugees being held at Guantánamo enter the United States.

FURTHER READING

General Accounts of Cuban American History

Boswell, Thomas D., and James R. Curtis. *The Cuban-American Experience: Culture, Images, and Perspectives.* Totowa, N.J.: Rowman & Allanheld, 1983.

Bretos, Miguel A. *Cuba and Florida: Exploration of an Historic Connection, 1539–1991.* Miami: Historical Association of Southern Florida, 1991.

de Varona, Frank, ed. *Hispanic Presence in the United States: Historical Beginnings.* Miami: Mnemosyne, 1993.

Henderson, Ann L., and Gary R. Mormino, eds. *Spanish Pathways in Florida: 1492–1992.* Sarasota, Fla.: Pineapple Press, 1991.

Heyck, Denis Lynn Daly. *Barrios and Borderlands: Cultures of Latinos and Latinas in the United States.* New York: Routledge, 1994.

Olson, James S., and Judith E. Olson. *Cuban Americans: From Trauma to Triumph.* New York: Twayne, 1995.

Poyo, Gerald E., and Mariano Díaz-Miranda. "Cubans in the United States." In *Handbook of Hispanic Culture in the United States,* edited by Alfredo Jiménez. Houston: Arte Publico Press, 1994.

Rieff, David. *Going to Miami: Exiles, Tourists, and Refugees in the New America.* Boston: Little, Brown, 1987.

———. *The Exile: Cuba in the Heart of Miami.* New York: Simon & Schuster, 1993.

Specific Aspects of Cuban American History

Allman, T. D. *Miami: City of the Future.* New York: The Atlantic Monthly Press, 1987.

de Onís, Juan, and Federico de Onís, eds. *The America of José Martí.* New York: Minerva Press, 1954.

Mormino, Gary R., and George E. Pozzetta. *The Immigrant World of Ybor City.* Urbana: University of Illinois Press, 1987.

Pérez Firmat, Gustavo. *Life on the Hyphen: The Cuban-American Way.* Austin: University of Texas Press, 1994.

Portes, Alejandro, and Alex Stepich. *City on the Edge: The Transformation of Miami.* Berkeley: University of California Press, 1993.

Prieto, Yolanda. "Cuban Women in New Jersey: Gender Relations and Change." In *Seeking Common Ground: Multidisciplinary Studies of Immigrant Women in the United States,* edited by Donna Gabaccia. Westport, Conn.: Greenwood, 1992.

Westfall, L. Glenn. *Key West: Cigar City U.S.A.* Key West, Fla.: The Historic Key West Preservation Board, 1986.

Personal Accounts of Cuban American Life

Arnaz, Desi. *A Book.* New York: William Morrow, 1976.

Banks, Ann, ed. *First Person America.* New York: Knopf, 1980.

Bode, Janet. *New Kids on the Block.* New York: Franklin Watts, 1989.

Dolan, Terry, Janet Satterfield, and Chris Stade, eds. *A Road Well Traveled: Three Generations of Cuban American Women.* Newton, Mass.: Women's Educational Equity Act Program, U.S. Department of Education, 1988.

Franqui, Carlos. *Family Portrait with Fidel: A Memoir.* New York: Vintage, 1985.

Garver, Susan, and Paula McGuire. *Coming to North America: From Mexico, Cuba, and Puerto Rico.* New York: Delacorte, 1981.

Geldof, Lynn. *Cubans: Voices of Change.* New York: St. Martin's, 1991.

Hospital, Carolina, ed. *Cuban American Writers: Los Atrevidos.* Princeton: Linden Land Press, 1988.

Medina, Pablo. *Exiled Memories: A Cuban Childhood.* Austin: University of Texas Press, 1990.

Morrison, Joan, and Charlotte Fox Zabusky. *American Mosaic: The Immigrant Experience in the Words of Those Who Lived It.* Pittsburgh: The University of Pittsburgh Press, 1980.

Namias, June. *First Generation.* Boston: Beacon, 1978.

Owsley, Beatrice Rodriguez. *The Hispanic-American Entrepreneur: An Oral History of the American Dream.* New York: Twayne, 1992.

Pérez Firmat, Gustavo. *Next Year in Cuba: A Cubano's Coming-of-Age in America.* New York: Doubleday/Anchor Books, 1995.

Philipson, Lorrin, and Rafael Llerena. *Freedom Flights: Cuban Refugees Talk about Life under Castro and How They Fled His Regime.* New York: Random House, 1980.

Santoli, Al. *New Americans: An Oral History.* New York: Viking, 1988.

TEXT CREDITS

Main Text

p. 12, top: "Life History of Jose Ramon Sanfeliz," typescript, Bureau of Florida Folklife, Florida Department of State, Collection of Works Progress Administration interviews, 1-2.

p. 12, bottom: Esteban Montejo, *The Autobiography of a Runaway Slave,* ed. Miguel Barne (New York: Meridian, 1969), 153-54.

p. 13, top: Desi Arnaz, *A Book* (New York: William Morrow, 1976), 12-13. Reprinted by permission of the William Morris Agency, Inc. on behalf of the author. Copyright © 1976 by Desi Arnaz.

p. 13, bottom: Interview with Digna Olga-Blanco, conducted by Dorothy Hoobler, March 22, 1995.

p. 14: From *Exiled Memories: A Cuban Childhood* by Pablo Medina, Copyright © 1990. By permission of the University of Texas Press. Pp. 38-39.

p. 15: Ruth Behar, "Juban America," *Poetics Today*, author's prepublication copy, galley 94.

p. 16: Interview with Rosa Vazquez, conducted by Dorothy Hoobler, January 31, 1995.

p. 17, top: Interview with Margarita Sainz de la Peña Gagliardi, conducted by Dorothy Hoobler, March 6, 1995.

p. 17, bottom: Interview with Hamlet Arias, conducted by Thomas Hoobler, March 29, 1995.

p. 18, top: Ellis Island Oral History Project: Margo Nash interview with Tamahra Calzadilla.

p. 18, bottom: From *Exiled Memories: A Cuban Childhood* by Pablo Medina, Copyright © 1990. By permission of the University of Texas Press. Pp. 108-10.

p. 20: Janet Bode, *New Kids on the Block* (New York: Franklin Watts, 1989), 46-47.

p. 21: Excerpted with permission of Twayne Publishers, an imprint of Simon & Schuster Macmillan, from *The Hispanic-American Entrepreneur: An Oral History of the American Dream* by Beatrice Rodriguez Owsley. Copyright © 1992 by Twayne Publishers. Pp. 15-16.

p. 22, top: Excerpted with permission of Twayne Publishers, an imprint of Simon & Schuster Macmillan, from *The Hispanic- American Entrepreneur: An Oral History of the American Dream* by Beatrice Rodriguez Owsley. Copyright © 1992 by Twayne Publishers. Page 30.

p. 22, middle: Terry Dolan, Janet Satterfield, and Chris Stade, eds., *A Road Well Traveled: Three Generations of Cuban American Women* (Newton, Mass.: Women's Educational Equity Act Program, U.S. Department of Education, 1988), 48.

p. 22, bottom: Giles R. Wright, *The Reasons for Migrating* (Trenton, N.J.: New Jersey Historical Commission, 1986), 21.

p. 23, top: Reprinted from *American Mosaic: The Immigrant Experience in the Words of Those Who Lived It,* by Joan Morrison and Charlotte Fox Zabusky, © 1980, 1993, by permission of the University of Pittsburgh Press, 324-25.

p. 23, middle: Dolan et al., *A Road Well Traveled,* 66.

p. 23, bottom: June Namias, *First Generation* (Boston: Beacon, 1978), 158.

p. 24, top: Reprinted from *American Mosaic: The Immigrant Experience in the Words of Those Who Lived It,* by Joan Morrison and Charlotte Fox Zabusky, © 1980, 1993, by permission of the University of Pittsburgh Press, 321.

p. 24, bottom: Susan Garver and Paula McGuire, *Coming to North America: From Mexico, Cuba, and Puerto Rico* (New York: Delacorte, 1981), 88.

p. 25, top: Interview with Mike Yip, conducted by Dorothy and Thomas Hoobler, February 23, 1995.

p. 25, bottom: Lorrin Philipson and Rafael Llerena, *Freedom Flights: Cuban Refugees Talk About Life under Castro and How They Fled His Regime* (New York: Random House, 1980), 127.

p. 30, top: Gustavo Pérez Firmat, *Next Year in Cuba: A Cubano's Coming-of-Age in America* (New York: Doubleday/Anchor Books, 1995), 17-18.

p. 30, bottom: Flora González Mandri, *The Day We Left,* trans. Beth Wellington, work in progress © 1995 by Flora González Mandri, 1-4.

p. 31: Excerpted with permission of Twayne Publishers, an imprint of Simon & Schuster Macmillan, from *The Hispanic-American Entrepreneur: An Oral History of the American Dream* by Beatrice Rodriguez Owsley. Copyright © 1992 by Twayne Publishers. Page 82.

p. 32, top: Interview with Margarita Sainz de la Peña Gagliardi, conducted by Dorothy Hoobler, March 6, 1995.

p. 32, bottom: Reprinted from *American Mosaic: The Immigrant Experience in the Words of Those Who Lived It,* by Joan Morrison and Charlotte Fox Zabusky, © 1980, 1993, by permission of the University of Pittsburgh Press, 320-22.

p. 33: Dolan et al., *A Road Well Traveled,* 141, 144.

p. 34: Maria Luisa Salcines, author's manuscript, 2-3.

p. 35: Philipson and Llerena, *Freedom Flights,* 82-86.

p. 36: Philipson and Llerena, *Freedom Flights,* 65-67.

p. 37: Interview with Hamlet Arias, conducted by Thomas Hoobler, March 29, 1995.

p. 40: Hamilton Holt, ed., *The Life Stories of Undistinguished Americans* (New York: Routledge, 1990), 187-88.

p. 41: Bernardo Vega, *Memoirs of Bernardo Vega* (New York: Monthly Review Press, 1984), 59-61, 65-66.

p. 42: "Personal History of Dr. M. Santos," taken by F. Valdes, typescript, Bureau of Florida Folklife, Florida Department of State, Collection of Works Progress Administration interviews, 1-3.

p. 43: "Life History of Mr. Pedro Barrios," taken by F. Valdes, typescript, Bureau of Florida Folklife, Florida Department of State, Collection of Works Progress Administration interviews, 3-4, 6-8.

p. 44, top: From *Exiled Memories: A Cuban Childhood* by Pablo Medina, Copyright © 1990. By permission of the University of Texas Press. Page 1.

p. 44, bottom: Cristina Garcia, "Growing Up Latin," *Cosmopolitan,* November 1994, 222. Reprinted by permission of Ellen Levine Literary Agency. Copyright © 1994 by Cristina Garcia.

p. 45: Interview with Margarita Sainz de la Peña Gagliardi, conducted by Dorothy Hoobler, March 6, 1995.

p. 46, top: Dolan et al., *A Road Well Traveled,* 77.

p. 46, bottom: Namias, *First Generation,* 159.

p. 47, top: Philipson and Llerena, *Freedom Flights,* 38-39.

p. 47, bottom: Interview with Hamlet Arias, conducted by Thomas Hoobler, March 29, 1995.

p. 48, top: Desi Arnaz, *A Book* (New York: William Morrow, 1976), 33-34. Reprinted by permission of the William Morris Agency, Inc. on behalf of the author. Copyright © 1976 by Desi Arnaz.

p. 48, bottom: Marisella Veiga, "The Day I Learned English," author's manuscript, 1-2.

p. 49: Dolan et al., *A Road Well Traveled,* 90-91.

p. 50: Pérez Firmat, *Next Year in Cuba,* 157.

p. 51: Interview with Rosa Vazquez, conducted by Dorothy Hoobler, January 31, 1995.

p. 52, top: Dolan et al., *A Road Well Traveled,* 26.

p. 52, middle: Reprinted from *American Mosaic: The Immigrant Experience in the Words of Those Who Lived It,* by Joan Morrison and Charlotte Fox Zabusky, © 1980, 1993, by permission of the University of Pittsburgh Press, 326.

p. 52, bottom: Dolan et al., *A Road Well Traveled,* 144.

p. 53: Dolan et al., *A Road Well Traveled,* 77-78.

p. 58, top: "Life History of Domingo Ginesta," typescript, Bureau of Florida Folklife, Florida Department of State, Collection of Works Progress Administration interviews, 2-3.

p. 58, bottom: Louis A. Pérez, Jr. "Reminiscences of a *Lector*: Cuban Cigar Workers in Tampa," *Tampa Bay History* 7 (Fall/Winter 1985): 137-40.

p. 61: Nancy A. Hewitt, "Women in Ybor City: An Interview with a Woman Cigarworker," *Tampa Bay History* 7 (Fall/Winter 1985): 162-64.

p. 62: "Interview Obtained by Mr. Valdes," typescript, Bureau of Florida Folklife, Florida Department of State, Collection of Works Progress Administration interviews, 1-2.

p. 63: José Yglesias, "The Radical Latino Island in the Deep South," *Tampa Bay History* 7 (Fall/Winter 1985): 168-69.

p. 64, top: Lynn Geldof, *Cubans: Voices of Change* (New York: St. Martin's, 1991), 199-200.

p. 64, middle: David Rieff, *The Exile: Cuba in the Heart of Miami* (New York: Simon & Schuster, 1993), 81.

p. 64, bottom: Namias, *First Generation,* 161-62.

p. 65: Dolan et al., *A Road Well Traveled,* 66-67.

p. 66: "The Blue-Eyed Cuban," from *New Americans: An Oral History* by Al Santoli. Copyright © 1988 by Al Santoli. Used by permission of Viking Penguin, a division of Penguin Books USA Inc. Page 377.

p. 67, top: Dolan et al., *A Road Well Traveled,* 144-45.

p. 67, middle: Dolan et al., *A Road Well Traveled,* 133-34.

p. 67, bottom: Yolanda Prieto, "Cuban Women in New Jersey: Gender Relations and Change," in *Seeking Common Ground: Multidisciplinary Studies of Immigrant Women in the United States,* ed. Donna Gabaccia, (Westport, Conn.: Greenwood, 1992), 187-88.

p. 68: Pérez Firmat, *Next Year in Cuba,* 80.

p. 69, top: Alejandro Portes and Alex Stepich, *City on the Edge: The Transformation of Miami* (Berkeley: University of California Press, 1993), 36.

p. 69, bottom: Interview with Mike Yip, conducted by Dorothy and Thomas Hoobler, February 23, 1995.

p. 70: Excerpted with permission of Twayne Publishers, an imprint of Simon & Schuster Macmillan, from *The Hispanic-American Entrepreneur: An Oral History of the American Dream* by Beatrice Rodriguez Owsley. Copyright © 1992 by Twayne Publishers. Pp. 86-87.

p. 71, top: Dolan et al., *A Road Well Traveled,* 82.

p. 71, bottom: Dolan et al., *A Road Well Traveled,* 124.

p. 72: Excerpted with permission of Twayne Publishers, an imprint of Simon & Schuster Macmillan, from *The Hispanic-American Entrepreneur: An Oral History of the American Dream* by Beatrice Rodriguez Owsley. Copyright © 1992 by Twayne Publishers. Pp. 82-83.

p. 73: Interview with Dr. Rosa Vazquez, conducted by Dorothy Hoobler, January 31, 1995.

p. 74, top: Cristina Garcia, "Growing Up Latin," *Cosmopolitan,* November 1994, 222. Reprinted by permission of Ellen Levine Literary Agency. Copyright © 1994 by Cristina Garcia.

p. 74, bottom: Dolan et al., *A Road Well Traveled,* 31-32.

p. 75, top: "The Blue-Eyed Cuban," from *New Americans: An Oral History* by Al Santoli. Copyright © 1988 by Al Santoli. Used by permission of Viking Penguin, a division of Penguin Books USA Inc. Page 385.

p. 75, bottom: Dolan et al., *A Road Well Traveled,* 128-29.

p. 80, top: Rieff, *The Exile,* 30-31.

p. 80, bottom: Pérez Firmat, *Next Year in Cuba,* 64-65.

p. 81: Dolan et al., *A Road Well Traveled,* 139-40.

p. 82, top: "Union City and Miami: A Sisterhood Born of Cuban Roots," *New York Times,* November 30, 1992, section B.

p. 82, bottom: Interview with Barry Moreno, conducted by Dorothy Hoobler, February 14, 1995.

p. 83, top: Geldof, *Cubans: Voices of Change,* 194.

p. 83, bottom: Interview with Hamlet Arias, conducted by Thomas Hoobler, March 29, 1995.

p. 84: Yglesias, "The Radical Latino Island in the Deep South," 167-68.

p. 85: Dolan et al., *A Road Well Traveled*, 106.

p. 86: Rieff, *The Exile*, 54-55.

p. 87, top: Rieff, *The Exile,* 134.

p. 87, bottom: Rieff, *The Exile,* 135-36.

p. 88, top: Interview with Dr. Rosa Vazquez, conducted by Dorothy Hoobler, January 31, 1995.

p. 88, bottom: Cristina Garcia, "Growing Up Latin," *Cosmopolitan,* November 1994, 223. Reprinted by permission of Ellen Levine Literary Agency. Copyright © 1994 by Cristina Garcia.

p. 89: Namias, *First Generation,* 162.

p. 90, top: Marifeli Pérez-Stable, "Culture-Maker: Oscar Hijuelos," *culturefront* (Winter 1993), published by the New York Council for the Humanities, 17-19.

p. 90, bottom: Dolan et al., *A Road Well Traveled,* 109-10.

p. 91: Maria Luisa Salcines, author's manuscript, 7, 10-11.

p. 92, top: Gustavo Pérez Firmat, *Life on the Hyphen: The Cuban-American Way* (Austin: University of Texas Press, 1994), 5.

p. 92, bottom: Dolan et al., *A Road Well Traveled,* 79.

p. 94: From *Exiled Memories: A Cuban Childhood* by Pablo Medina, Copyright © 1990. By permission of the University of Texas Press. Pp. 2-3.

p. 95: Dolan et al., *A Road Well Traveled,* 134-35.

p. 96: Ray Gonzalez, ed., *Currents from the Dancing River* (San Diego: Harcourt Brace, 1994), 89.

p. 97: Maria Luisa Salcines, *The Monitor* (McAllen, Tex.), January 9, 1995.

p. 98: Carolina Hospital, author's manuscript, 1-2.

p. 99, top: Interview with Barry Moreno, conducted by Dorothy Hoobler, February 14, 1995.

p. 99, bottom: Interview with Rosa Vazquez, conducted by Dorothy Hoobler, January 31, 1995.

p. 100, top: Reprinted from *American Mosaic: The Immigrant Experience in the Words of Those Who Lived It,* by Joan Morrison and Charlotte Fox Zabusky, © 1980, 1993, by permission of the University of Pittsburgh Press, 327.

p. 100, bottom: Marifeli Pérez-Stable, "Culture-Maker: Cristina Garcia," *culturefront* (Winter 1993), published by the New York Council for the Humanities, 11.

p. 101: Pérez Firmat, *Next Year in Cuba,* 72-74.

p. 102, top: Dolan, et al., *A Road Well Traveled,* 118.

p. 102, bottom: Flora González Mandri, *The House on Lopez Recio Street,* trans. Angela McEwain, Jaime Martínez-Tolentino, and the author; work in progress © 1995 by Flora González Mandri, 10, 13-15.

p. 108, top: Excerpted with permission of Twayne Publishers, an imprint of Simon & Schuster Macmillan, from *The Hispanic-American Entrepreneur: An Oral History of the American Dream* by Beatrice Rodriguez Owsley. Copyright © 1992 by Twayne Publishers. Page 18.

p. 108, bottom: Marisella Veiga, "A First Identity: One of Many Losses," author's manuscript, 2-5.

p. 109: Pérez Firmat, *Next Year in Cuba,* 9-10.

p. 110, top: Maria Luisa Salcines, *The Monitor* (McAllen, Tex.), September 8, 1994, page 7.

p. 110, bottom: "The Blue-Eyed Cuban," from *New Americans: An Oral History* by Al Santoli. Copyright © 1988 by Al Santoli. Used by permission of Viking Penguin, a division of Penguin Books USA Inc. Page 369.

p. 111, top: Excerpted with permission of Twayne Publishers, an imprint of Simon & Schuster Macmillan, from *The Hispanic-American Entrepreneur: An Oral History of the American Dream* by Beatrice Rodriguez Owsley. Copyright © 1992 by Twayne Publishers. Pp. 83-84.

p. 111, bottom: Cristina Garcia, "Growing Up Latin," *Cosmopolitan,* November 1994, 223. Reprinted by permission of Ellen Levine Literary Agency. Copyright © 1994 by Cristina Garcia.

p. 112: Desi Arnaz, *A Book* (New York: William Morrow, 1976), 59, 61-62. Reprinted by permission of the William Morris Agency, Inc. on behalf of the author. Copyright © 1976 by Desi Arnaz.

p. 113: Interview with Digna Olga-Blanco, conducted by Dorothy Hoobler, March 22, 1995.

p. 114: Excerpted with permission of Twayne Publishers, an imprint of Simon & Schuster Macmillan, from *The Hispanic-American Entrepreneur: An Oral History of the American Dream* by Beatrice Rodriguez Owsley. Copyright © 1992 by Twayne Publishers. Page 46.

p. 115: Interview with Rosa Vazquez, conducted by Dorothy Hoobler, January 31, 1995.

p. 116: Dolan et al., *A Road Well Traveled,* 70.

p. 117: Carolina Hospital, ed., *Cuban American Writers: Los Atrevidos* (Princeton, N.J.: Linden Lane, 1988), 15.

Sidebars

p. 17: David Rieff, *The Exile: Cuba in the Heart of Miami* (New York: Simon & Schuster, 1993), 80.

p. 21: Alejandro Portes and Alex Stepich, *City on the Edge: The Transformation of Miami* (Berkeley: University of California Press, 1993), 99.

p. 23: James A. Michener and John Kings, *Six Days in Havana* (Austin: University of Texas Press, 1989), 29-30.

p. 82: Portes and Stepich, *City on the Edge,* 114.

p. 115: Marifeli Pérez-Stable, *culturefront* (Winter 1993), published by the New York Council for the Humanities, 69.

PICTURE CREDITS

Archdiocese of Miami: 75; Archive Photos: 15 top, 16 top, 16 bottom, 18, 20 top, 20 bottom, 21, 23, 24, 25, 35 top, 112; Tony Arruza: 65, 66, 70, 73, 87, 101, 108 bottom, 109; courtesy of Lourdes Bauza, print by Barbara Ernzerhoff: 14, 115; Julio Bulnes: cover, frontispiece, 79; Cuban-American Student Association, University of Florida: 111; from E. de Varona family album: 22 top, 76, 91, 92 top; Frank and Haydee de Varona: 118, 119, 120, 121; Florida Department of Commerce, Division of Tourism: 100 top (Robert Overton), 114; Florida State Archives: 14 top, 41 bottom, 42 top, 52, 57, 69 top, 72; courtesy of the Fort Lauderdale Historical Society, Inc. (Gene Hyde Collection): 44 bottom; Margarita Sainz de la Peña Gagliardi: 31 top, 31 bottom, 49 top; Flora González Mandri: 49 bottom; Greater Miami Convention and Visitors Bureau: 106, 107; courtesy of Oscar Hijuelos: 6, 7; courtesy of the Hispanic Society of America, New York: 8, 10, 13, 15 bottom, 17; Historical Association of Southern Florida: 19 bottom (gift of James Ernerman), 20 (Miami News Collection), 35 bottom (courtesy of Humberto Sanchez), 38 (Miami News Collection), 42 bottom, 44 top, 45 (Miami News Collection), 94, 116 bottom (Miami News Collection); Thomas Hoobler: 71 top; Carolina Hospital: 116 top; Justo A. Martí Photographic Collection, Centro de Estudios Puertorriqueños, Hunter College, City University of New York: 28, 56, 78, 81, 83 top, 83 bottom, 89 bottom, 92 bottom, 100 bottom, 113 bottom; Impact Visuals: 63; Wright Langley: 26, 37 bottom (USMC photo, G. M. Conroy), 40, 41 top, 43, 47, 64, 68, 82, 89 top, 95 top, 96, 108 top; courtesy of Lydia Lima, Oxford University Press: 93; Maria Lino: 86 top, 90 bottom; Monroe County Library, Key West, Florida: 58; Museum of the City of New York: 59 top; National Archives: 37 top; National Park Service: 5, 30 top, 32; Catherine Noren: 54, 67, 69 bottom, 86 bottom; Ohlinger: 113 top, 117 top; Reuters/Bettmann: 34, 36 bottom, 46 bottom, 50 bottom; Maria Luisa Salcines: 36 top, 51, 90 top; courtesy of Tampa-Hillsborough County Public Library System: 59 bottom; Cuban Archives, Otto G. Richter Library, University of Miami, Coral Gables, Florida: 12, 22 bottom, 30 bottom, 33, 71 bottom, 84 top, 84 bottom, 85, 97, 110, 117 bottom; Special Collections Department, University of South Florida Library: 60 top, 60 bottom, 61, 62, 80 top, 80 bottom, 88; UPI/Bettmann: 46 top, 48, 50 top, 53, 74, 95 bottom, 98, 102, 103 bottom, 104; U.S. Coast Guard: 29; Marisella Veiga: 11, 99 top, 99 bottom.

INDEX

Page numbers in *italics* indicate illustrations.

ACKNOWLEDGMENTS

We have been overwhelmed by the generosity of many people who helped us assemble the accounts and illustrations in this book. First, Carolina Hospital kindly provided some of her written work and suggested sources of information on the Cuban American experience. Her advice was particularly valuable in putting us in touch with others in the Cuban American community. Maria Luisa Salcines and Marisella Veiga wrote essays especially for this book, and our only regret is that we did not have space to publish them in their entirety. All three of these talented writers also provided pictures. Our deep thanks to them.

Gustavo Pérez Firmat graciously provided galleys from his book *Next Year in Cuba: A Cubano's Coming-of-Age.* Flora González Mandri provided material from *The Day We Left,* a work in progress. Ruth Behar also generously shared the galleys for her new article, "Juban America." Dr. Graciella Beecher kindly assisted us with suggestions for first-person material. Many thanks to Bishop Agustín Román, who provided an account of his life and work. Maria de los Angeles Torres shared information on the Pedro Pan program from her research for a work in progress. Thanks also to Lourdes Bauza, who invited us to her home to share photographs and memories about her husband, Mario Bauza. Yolanda Prieto, Dr. Paul George, and Dr. Uva Clavijo also provided names of useful contacts.

Esperanza de Varona provided research and many pictures for us from the collection of the Otto G. Richter Library at the University of Miami. She went well beyond the call of duty in responding to requests from us. Many thanks.

Barry Moreno allowed us to interview him and guided us through the oral history collection of the Statue of Liberty/Ellis Island National Monument. Others who generously gave their time in retelling their life histories were Hamlet Arias, Dr. Rosa Vazquez, Digna Winter, Mike Yip, and Margarita Sainz de la Peña Gagliardi. We owe special thanks to Margarita Gagliardi for trusting us with the passport that allowed her to leave Cuba.

Among the many people who provided us with photographs for this book are Tony Arruza; Julio Bulnes; Paul Eugen Camp of the Special Collections division of the Library of the University of South Florida; Barbara Ernzerhoff; Oliver and Janet Garcia; Susan Gillis of the Fort Lauderdale Historical Society; Tom Hambright of the May Hill Russell Library in Key West; Pedro Juan Hernández, archivist at the Centro de Estudios Puertorriqueños, Hunter College; Dawn Hugh of the Historical Association of Southern Florida; Kurt E. Jasielonis of the Tampa-Hillsborough County Public Library; Wright Langley of Langley Press; Patrick Lenaghan of the Hispanic Society of America; Lydia Lima; Maria Lino; Dixie Lee Nims of the Florida Department of Commerce Division of Tourism; Catherine Noren; Joanna Norman and Joan Morse of the Florida State Archives; Robert Overton; Tony Pisani of the Museum of the City of New York; and Michael Shulman and Michael Orlick at Archive Photos. We are particularly grateful to Humberto Sanchez, who collects artifacts of the Cuban migration to the United States, for giving permission to use one of his photographs.

We also owe thanks to Mora Byrd of the Caribbean Culture Center in New York City; Michelle Brent of the Tampa/Hillsborough Convention and Visitors Association; Rusty N. Ennemoser of the Florida Department of State Division of Historical Resources; Bill Mansfield of the Florida Folklife Program; Raimondo Rey of the Living History Project at Florida International University; Jeanne Sullivan of the Greater Miami Convention and Visitors Bureau; and our editors at Oxford University Press, Tara Deal and Nancy Toff.

Finally, we wish to express our deep gratitude to Frank and Haydee de Varona for opening the pages of their own Cuban American family album and sharing their memories with us. Throughout the writing of this book, we have benefited from Frank's sound advice and from the published works that he has written. *¡Muchas gracias!*

ABOUT THE AUTHORS

Dorothy and Thomas Hoobler have published more than 60 books for children and young adults, including *Vietnam: Why We Fought; Mexican Portraits; Latin American Portraits;* and *Latin America.* Their works have been honored by the Society for School Librarians International, the Library of Congress, the New York Public Library, the National Council for Social Studies, and *Best Books for Children,* among other organizations and publications. The Hooblers have also written several volumes of historical fiction for children, including *Next Stop Freedom, Frontier Diary, The Summer of Dreams,* and *Treasure in the Stream.* Dorothy Hoobler received her master's degree in American history from New York University and worked as a textbook editor before becoming a full-time free-lance editor and writer. Thomas Hoobler received his master's degree in education from Xavier University and has worked as a teacher and textbook editor.